ARMS & ARMOUR
of the English Civil Wars

David Blackmore

ROYAL
ARMOURIES

Introduction

The causes of the English Civil Wars are many and complex. They concerned the rights of the king, Charles I to levy taxes, the fear of re-establishment of Catholicism and Parliament's demands for an increased role in the government of the country. These causes and the series of events leading up to the outbreak of war have been well rehearsed by many historians and are beyond the scope of this introduction.

There were, in fact, three separate wars (the first from 1642 to 1646, the second in 1648, and the third from 1649 to 1651). It is curious that despite the great number of books published about this period none has dealt to any extent with the arms and armour in use. This publication is intended to go some way to supplying that want.

The English Civil Wars were the first major armed conflict the country had been involved in since the war against Spain, 1585 to 1603, and the defeat of the Armada in 1588. Apart from a few unsuccessful forays on the continent and, for Charles I, the disasterous campaigns against the Scots, the country had remained at peace at a time when the continent was being ravaged by the Thirty Years War. Because of this England was far from prepared for war. Apart from a few garrisons there were no standing forces to speak of and the militia was in a state of almost total ineffectiveness, with the notable exception of the London Trained Bands who were to serve Parliament so well at the start of the wars. At that time, however, many English gentlemen and nobles had gained experience of war by volunteering to serve in the various armies fighting throughout Europe. These men were able to pass on to the hurriedly raised forces of king and Parliament the benefit of their experience and many, like Sir William Waller and Lord Hopton, became notable commanders. It is one of the sad ironies of these wars that Waller and Hopton commanded armies on opposing sides and clashed frequently yet had not only served together on the continent but were great friends. Another Englishman versed in the art of war was the Earl of Essex, who led Parliament's first army against the king. Many others, however, had no experience at all of warfare. Perhaps the best known example of this is Oliver Cromwell, a country squire who rose from the rank of Captain to Lord-General. As a result of this situation the officer corps of both sides contained a similar mix of amateurs and professionals, in that respect at least the forces of king and Parliament were equally supplied.

The official date for the start of the English Civil Wars is 22nd August 1642 when Charles I raised the Royal Standard at Nottingham. Prior to that, however, there had been much manoeuvering and even skirmishing from as early as May when Sir Francis Wortley began to raise troops for the king. During those first months of conflict one of the main objectives of both sides was control of the various county magazines that held the arms of the militia. When Sir John Hotham denied the king entry into Hull inApril it was to prevent the magazine, the most important in England after the Tower of London, falling into the king's hands. Charles did, however, gain control of a number of the smaller militia magazines and was able to 'borrow' the arms of several northern militia units. These and arms supplied by some of the great nobles were the only sources of arms available to the king at the outbreak of war.

Parliament, on the other hand, gained control of the Tower of London and the important magazines at Portsmouth and Hull. Parliament also controlled the navy and thus the arms it had. The importance of the Tower as a store of arms for immediate use at the beginning of the war should not be overated. In January 1642 the Lieutenant of the Ordnance wrote, 'very shortly there will be little cause to stand in awe of the Tower, for all the arms almost are already issued out for Ireland and non brought in to replenish the Magazine.' By April the store held only 1,367 muskets and 354 pikes. In May Parliament ordered the transfer of the Hull magazine to London in a move to improve the situation. However the Tower's great importance lay in the fact that it was the nerve centre of the military production and supply system of the country. Because of that most of England's arms manufacturing industry was based in London. Although some initial confusion was caused by the departure, to join the King, of some senior figures in the office of the Ordnance, the government department with its headquarters in the Tower responsible for the supply of military material, Parliament's control of that office and the London arms industry was to prove invaluable in the long run.

At the beginning of the war, then, both sides suffered from a chronic shortage of arms and both attempted to solve the problem by imports from the continent. For the king his seizure of

Figure 4
English cuirassier helmet opened up
to show the constituent parts.
Royal Armouries IV 1026.

Figure 5
Todenkopf or Savoyard form of
cuirassier headpiece. This helmet is
fastened by means of a strap rather
than a swivel-hook.
Royal Armouries IV 48.

the breastplate and are held in place by swivel
hooks, in this case on the straps, which locate into
the pierced lugs. The other, narrower, straps
which in the sixteenth century would have been
fixed to the gorget, secure the arm defences to the
backplate by means of the buckles on the
pauldrons. Also clearly shown is the way in which
the tassets, which protect the legs, are attached by
hinges with removable pins to each side of the gard
de reine, or culet, which protects the lower back.
This whole arrangement rests on the wide flanges
of the back and breastplates, secured at the rear by
a hook engaging in a stud on the backplate which
passes through the culet, and at the front by a
short belt. When being worn the angle of the
backplate to the culet prevents the pins of the two
hinges from slipping out. Two other methods of
securing the tassets were in use at this time. In one
method each tasset was fixed to the flange of the
breastplate by a bolt and a wing-nut whilst in the
other each tasset was pierced at the top by a keyhole slot which fitted over a mushroom-headed
rivet on the flange of the breastplate and the tassets
were joined to each other by means of a short strap
and buckle (Figure 6). It is often possible to
shorten the length of the tassets by removing the
lower parts. In such cases the tassets are
constructed in two or three sections, which are
held together by a combination of turning pins and
mushroom-headed rivets and keyhole slots.

At this period most cuirassier armours ended at
the knee and the protection of the lower leg and
foot was left to the thick leather riding boot. A
number of armours did, however, continue to be
made with greaves, to protect the lower leg, and
sabatons, to protect the foot. These were made to
be worn over the square toed riding boot and as a
result are generally rather large and shapeless. An
example of this is the gilt armour of Charles I
made in 1612. (Colour plate 1).

By the time of the civil wars the arm and shoulder
defences of cuirassier armours were permanently
joined together, only the gauntlets being separate.
In order to make it possible to slide the arm into
the vambrace as it was known, the cannon, or
forearm defence, was made in two parts hinged
longitudinally at the back and closed by a simple
pin catch which depends on the natural spring in
the steel plates. The gauntlets are finely articulated
pieces of armour with flaring cuffs, usually pointed
and with thumb defences joined on by a small
hinge.

Introduction

The causes of the English Civil Wars are many and complex. They concerned the rights of the king, Charles I to levy taxes, the fear of re-establishment of Catholicism and Parliament's demands for an increased role in the government of the country. These causes and the series of events leading up to the outbreak of war have been well rehearsed by many historians and are beyond the scope of this introduction.

There were, in fact, three separate wars (the first from 1642 to 1646, the second in 1648, and the third from 1649 to 1651). It is curious that despite the great number of books published about this period none has dealt to any extent with the arms and armour in use. This publication is intended to go some way to supplying that want.

The English Civil Wars were the first major armed conflict the country had been involved in since the war against Spain, 1585 to 1603, and the defeat of the Armada in 1588. Apart from a few unsuccessful forays on the continent and, for Charles I, the disasterous campaigns against the Scots, the country had remained at peace at a time when the continent was being ravaged by the Thirty Years War. Because of this England was far from prepared for war. Apart from a few garrisons there were no standing forces to speak of and the militia was in a state of almost total ineffectiveness, with the notable exception of the London Trained Bands who were to serve Parliament so well at the start of the wars. At that time, however, many English gentlemen and nobles had gained experience of war by volunteering to serve in the various armies fighting throughout Europe. These men were able to pass on to the hurriedly raised forces of king and Parliament the benefit of their experience and many, like Sir William Waller and Lord Hopton, became notable commanders. It is one of the sad ironies of these wars that Waller and Hopton commanded armies on opposing sides and clashed frequently yet had not only served together on the continent but were great friends. Another Englishman versed in the art of war was the Earl of Essex, who led Parliament's first army against the king. Many others, however, had no experience at all of warfare. Perhaps the best known example of this is Oliver Cromwell, a country squire who rose from the rank of Captain to Lord-General. As a result of this situation the officer corps of both sides contained a similar mix of amateurs and professionals, in that respect at least the forces of king and Parliament were equally supplied.

The official date for the start of the English Civil Wars is 22nd August 1642 when Charles I raised the Royal Standard at Nottingham. Prior to that, however, there had been much manoeuvering and even skirmishing from as early as May when Sir Francis Wortley began to raise troops for the king. During those first months of conflict one of the main objectives of both sides was control of the various county magazines that held the arms of the militia. When Sir John Hotham denied the king entry into Hull inApril it was to prevent the magazine, the most important in England after the Tower of London, falling into the king's hands. Charles did, however, gain control of a number of the smaller militia magazines and was able to 'borrow' the arms of several northern militia units. These and arms supplied by some of the great nobles were the only sources of arms available to the king at the outbreak of war.

Parliament, on the other hand, gained control of the Tower of London and the important magazines at Portsmouth and Hull. Parliament also controlled the navy and thus the arms it had. The importance of the Tower as a store of arms for immediate use at the beginning of the war should not be overated. In January 1642 the Lieutenant of the Ordnance wrote, 'very shortly there will be little cause to stand in awe of the Tower, for all the arms almost are already issued out for Ireland and non brought in to replenish the Magazine.' By April the store held only 1,367 muskets and 354 pikes. In May Parliament ordered the transfer of the Hull magazine to London in a move to improve the situation. However the Tower's great importance lay in the fact that it was the nerve centre of the military production and supply system of the country. Because of that most of England's arms manufacturing industry was based in London. Although some initial confusion was caused by the departure, to join the King, of some senior figures in the office of the Ordnance, the government department with its headquarters in the Tower responsible for the supply of military material, Parliament's control of that office and the London arms industry was to prove invaluable in the long run.

At the beginning of the war, then, both sides suffered from a chronic shortage of arms and both attempted to solve the problem by imports from the continent. For the king his seizure of

Newcastle and early capture of Bristol were of paramount importance for this. From the very beginning of the war arms from Holland and France were brought in through Newcastle. Parliament of course controlled London, the greatest port of all, and a large proportion of the arms issued to the Earl of Essex's army in 1642 came from abroad.

However, the importation of arms was expensive and often the arms so acquired were of doubtful quality. Furthermore the arms that could be seized from various magazines or given up by individuals were not enough to sustain a long drawn out war. Both sides had to look to home based arms manufacturing. At first glance it appears that Parliament with its control of the Tower and the London arms industry was in a vastly superior position to the king, but that is not entirely the case. The king controlled the Forest of Dean and South Wales, areas where iron was produced, and also the iron working areas of Shropshire, where one iron founder produced 44 cannon, and the West Midlands. These areas supplied much of the material the king needed to sustain his fight against Parliament. In Oxford, with the help of the officers of the Ordnance that had remained loyal, and local craftsmen, arms manufacturing began early in 1643. A cannon foundry was established in Christ Church using scrap metal, old cannon unfit for service and iron from the Forest of Dean. Sword production was also begun and powder-mills were set up. In addition to its value as a port Bristol also played its part as a centre of arms manufacturing. Just before it was captured by Parliament in 1645 it was reported as being capable of producing 15,000 muskets and 5,000 pikes in a year. The loss of Bristol was as fatal a blow to the king as his defeat at Naseby.

Parliament on the other hand might have controlled the Wealden iron industry but John Browne, the main supplier of cannon in the Weald, was a royalist sympathiser if not an active helper. The king's early attempt on London in 1642 resulted in the destruction of the country's main powder-mill in Surrey. The famous sword factory at Hounslow established in 1632 was confiscated from Benjamin Stone, its founder, because of his royalist connections, and converted to a powder-mill. Subsequently Parliament relied on Stone's bitter rivals, the London cutlers, for its swords. The king also controlled most of the country's coal producing areas and in 1643 a shortage of coal interrupted firearms manufacture

in London. There is no doubt that Parliament had an advantage over the king with regard to the supply of arms but it was by no means as great as is often believed. Those of the king's forces supplied from Oxford were well equipped, as were those parliamentarian forces that were supplied from London.

The great range of sources of arms and armour during the English Civil Wars means that the student of the period is faced with a tremendous variety amongst surviving material. But amongst arms manufactured in Britain there is a great deal of uniformity which is hardly surprising as, before the wars, all military arms were supposed to conform to patterns held by the Office of the Ordnance in the Tower of London. It followed that when war broke out and both sides were manufacturing their own arms they continued to produce what had been produced before. Even imports tended to come from the same countries. Because of this the arms and armour used by both sides were the same. The three-barred pott, for so long thought of as the Roundhead helmet, was in fact used by both sides. Indeed so similar were the troops of each side that clashes between forces on the same side were not unknown.

It is not possible in a publication of this size to cover all the variations of arms and armour that were employed during the English Civil Wars. Some things have had to be omitted. Scottish weapons of this period still had a very distinctive national style and their inclusion would have meant widening the scope of this publication beyond the limits of this format. Naval arms have also been omitted as the civil wars were primarily land affairs. What this publication seeks to do is inform the reader of the typical arms and armour of the period, how they were used, who made them, what they look like and what are their distinctive features.

Major sources are referred to in the text and bibliography. A full list is held in the Library of the Royal Armouries, HM Tower of London, and details may be obtained on application to the Librarian. Finally, the author would like to thank the Academic Committee of the Board of Trustees of the Armouries, A V B Norman and G M Wilson, successive Masters of the Armouries, and all his friends and colleagues at the Royal Armouries and elsewhere for their help and co-operation in the preparation of this work.

The CAVALRY

During the English Civil Wars most cavalry fell into one of two categories: the cuirassier and the harquebusier. The harquebusier was by far the more common of the two. Indeed, during the course of the wars, the cuirassier disappeared altogether.

The Cuirassier was the heavy cavalryman during the first half of the seventeenth century. Henry Hexham, quartermaster to the royalist Colonel Goring, has left us, in his *Principles*, published in Holland in 1642, a very detailed description, not only of the equipment of the cuirassier, but of the qualities required of both man and horse.

16. *Present and giue Fire.*

Figure 1
Cuirassier in action from John Cruso, Militaire Instructions for the Cavallrie, 1632.

'*In a cuirassier then is required, that he be a man of an able body, who is mounted upon a strong, and a lustie horse, that he hath on a good buff-gerkin, a short sword, or Coutlase by his side, a skarff about his armes, and bodie of his princes coullour, to distinguish him from his Ennemie coullour upon any service, or in the daie of battel.*

He ought to be mounted upon a strong, and a lustie horse, or Gelding, which is fiveteene palmes high . . . and likewise to be provided with a good Sadle, and Bridle, with two good pistolls hanging at his sadle bowe, in two strong pistoll Cases, the length of the pistoll barrils, being at the least foure and twenty ynches long, carrying a bullet of twentie in the pound, and of 24 which will roule in to his pistoll.

For his Armes about his bodie, he is first armed with a close helmet or a Cask pistoll proofe upon his head, 2. with a Gorget about his neck, 3. His brest and back peeces, which ought to be pistoll proofe, 4. His Pauldrons and vambraces his Guard de reines [culet], 5. His gauntles, 6. his tassets or thigh peeces reaching from his girdle beneath his knees, and (as is said) two pistols hanging at his saddle, and thus a Curassier is armed de cap en pied at all points even from the head to the foote.'

During the English Civil Wars relatively few cuirassier units were raised, but of those that were the parliamentarian, Sir Arthur Haselrigge's unit is probably the best known. Clarendon, in his *History of the Rebellion and Civil Wars in England*, wrote of them that they were

'*so prodigiously armed that they were called by the other side the regiment of lobsters because of the bright iron shells with which they were covered, being perfect cuirassiers; and were the first that made any impression on the kings horse, who being unarmed were not able to bear a shock with them; besides that they were secure from hurts of the sword, which were almost the only weapons the other were furnished with.*'

However, Haselrigge's Lobsters were defeated in 1643 at the battle of Roundway Down.

Nevertheless, the invulnerability of a cuirassier is graphically illustrated in Richard Atkyn's account of his personal duel with Haselrigge at that battle in *The Vindication of Richard Atkins*,

'Twas my fortune in a direct line to charge their General of Horse which I supposed to be so by his place. He discharged his carbine first but at a distance not to hurt us, and afterwards one of his pistols, before I came up to him and missed with both. I then immediately struck into him, and touched him before I discharged mine; and I'm sure I hit him, for he staggered and presently wheeled off from his party and ran . . .

. . . in six score yards I came up to him, and discharged the other pistol at him and I am sure I hit his head for I touched it before I gave fire and it amazed him at that present, but he was too well armed all over for a pistol bullet to do him any hurt, having a coat of mail over his arms and a headpiece (I am confident) musket proof.

In about six score more yards I came up to him again (having a very swift horse that Cornet Washnage gave me) and stuck by him a good while, and tried him from head to the saddle and could not penetrate him nor do him any hurt. But in this attempt he cut my horse's nose, that you might put your finger in the wound, and gave me such a blow on the inside of my arm amongst the veins that I could hardly hold my sword.'

'This story being related to the King at a second or third hand his answer was, 'Had he been victualled as well as fortified, he might have endured a siege of seven years'.

According to John Cruso in *Militarie Instructions for the Cavallrie*, the cuirassier originated in Germany where '. . . *when the Lanciers proved hard to be gotten . . . the cuirassier was invented, onely by discharging the lancier of his lance'*. The most important reason he gives for the replacement of the Lancer by the cuirassier, is that cuirassiers were more manoeuvrable than lancers. Other reasons were the shortage of properly trained men and horses and their expense.

However, despite the advantages of cuirassiers the few units that were raised did not survive for long. This was due as much to a general dislike of serving as a cuirassier, as to their lack of military success or any other considerations. Sir Edmund Verney wrote

'it will kill a man to serve in a whole cuirass. I am resolved to use nothing but back breast and gauntlet. If I had a pott for the head that were pistol proof it may be that I would use it, if it were light, but my whole helmet will be of no use to me at all'

Figure 2
Harquebusiers from John Cruso,
Militaire Instructions for the
Cavallrie, 1632.

Edmund Ludlow of Essex's lifeguard also discovered the drawbacks of serving as a cuirassier at Edgehill. *'Being dismounted'* he wrote, in his *Memoirs 'I could not without difficulty recover on horseback being loaded with cuirassiers arms, as the rest of the guard also were'*.

By far the most common type of cavalry used in the English Civil Wars was the harquebusier. This term was originally applied to lightly armoured cavalry, armed with an harquebus — a light, short barrelled firearm. By the time of the civil wars harquebusier had become a general term for all cavalry not equipped as cuirassier of lancers. As the smaller-bore carbine replaced the harquebus this type of cavalry was sometimes referred to as carbines. Once again very precise instructions as to their arming can be found in the military manuals of the day. To take one example, Vernon wrote in *The Young Horseman,*

'The Harquebus and Carbines arming is chiefly offensive, his defensive arms as only an open Caske or Headpiece, a back and breast with a buff-coat under his arms. His offensive arms are a good harquebus, [or] a carbine hanging on his right side in a belt by a swivel, a flask and cartridge case, and spanners and good firelock pistols in holsters. At his saddle a good stiffe sword sharp pointed and a good poll axe in his hand'.

As was so often the case, military theory differed from practice. From the very beginning harquebusiers appear to have worn either armour or a buff coat, not both. A document entitled *'Horse and Armes listed under Severall Captains of the Citty of London chiefly for the defence of the said cittye'* includes the following entry for the troop of one Captain Harvey.

'Abraham Chamberlaine of St Mary Axe listed two bay horses with starrs Armed with Carabines, pistolls with one buff coate the other with Back breast headpiece and Gauntlet, with two swords and poleaxes valued at 25 the piece in all fifty pounds.'

Another writer known only as JB wrote in an addition to William Barrife, *Militaire Discipline* (London 1661),

'But our late English wars neglected . . . cuirassiers and lancers making use of Harquebusiers. Armed only with a breast back and casque or pott for defence, a case of pistols short, and a carbine, hanging by a belt and swivel on his right side, of 2 or 2½ foot the length of the barrel and a good sword. Many troops and regiments only with sword and Pistol armed, their encounterings being not after the ancient manner of firing at a distance and wheeling off, which hath been found to be of dangerous consequence, but to fire at near distance their swords hanging at their wrists by a string, and with their sword points charging through the adverse troops'.

Indeed it seems clear that the cavalry raised by parliament was usually without buff-coats or carbines. An ordinance of Lords and Commons of September 1645 put the maximum value of the horse, furniture and arms of an harquebusier at £12 0s 0d. The total cost of horse, furniture, sword, pistols, armour and clothing when costed individually from other sources (and excluding carbines at about 12/9d and buff-coats which cost between £5 and £10), ranges from a minimum of £10/12/2d to a maximum of £12/12/10d. Furthermore, there are no surviving records of the supply of any buff-coats to any units of parliamentary cavalry and the issue of carbines is not common until 1650.

The situation in the royalist cavalry does not seem to have been too different. Clarendon wrote of them at the start of the war . . .

'Amongst the horse, the officers had their full desire if they were able to procure old backs and breasts and pots, with pistols or carbines for their two or three first ranks, and swords for the rest; themselves (and some soldiers by their examples) having gotten besides their pistols and swords, a short poleaxe.

The Earl of Essex, on the parliamentarian side, made a similar complaint

'The enemy's chief strength being in Horse and this Army neither recruited with Horses nor arms, nor saddles, it is impossible to keep the country from being plundered'.

An examinaton of the surviving Royalist Ordnance papers suggests that in general the only difference in the equipment of the cavalry of the two sides, in the main armies at least, was a tendency for the royalists to use more carbines, perhaps because of a shortage of pistols. Certainly Richard Atkyns who raised a troop for the King in 1643 does not seem to have experienced too much trouble equiping his men,

' . . . within one month, I mustered 60 men besides officers and almost all of them well armed. Master Dutton giving me 30 steel backs breasts and head pieces, and two men and horses completely armed . . .'

Prior to the English Civil Wars cavalry tactics had been greatly influenced by the German Reiters of the latter part of the sixteenth century. These troops depended upon firepower for their success, riding up to the enemy in successive ranks, firing their pistols and then retiring to reload. By the time the English Civil Wars broke out, however, the influence of the Swedish King Gustavus Adolphus, was already making itself felt. He formed his cavalry in three ranks, rather than the usual six for Reiter style tactics and taught them to charge home, reserving their fire for the mêlée. These tactics were employed by the royalist cavalry under Prince Rupert right from the beginning. His orders to the cavalry at Edge Hill are recorded by Sir Richard Bulstrode in his *Memoirs*,

> 'Just before we began our march Prince Rupert passed from one wing to the other giving positive orders to the horse, to march as close as possible, keeping their ranks with sword in hand, to receive the enemy's shot without firing either carbine or pistol till we broke in amongst the enemy, and then to make use of our firearms as need should require; which order was punctually observed'

Lord Bernard Stuart described what happened when the royalist horse charged the parliamentarians.

> . . . upon our approach they gave fire with their cannon lined amongst their horse, dragooners, carbines and pistols, but finding that did nothing dismay the King's horse, and that they came roundly to them with all their fire reserved, just when our men charged they all began to turn head.'

The parliamentarian cavalry, however, continued to rely upon firepower and this had disasterous consequences for them at Chalgrove Field in 1644. Prince Rupert was retiring to Oxford when he was caught by a large force of parliamentarian cavalry and turned to attack his pursuers. A contemporary account describes the cavalry battle that followed.

> 'Meantime Lieutenant-Colonell O'Neale having passed with the Princes regiment beyond the end of the hedge on the left hand, had begun the encounter with eight troopes of rebels. These having before seene ours facing about, took themselves off their speed presently, and made a fair stand till ours advanced up to charge them. So that they being first in order gave us their first vollie of carbines and pistols at a distance, as ours were advancing: yea they had time for their second pistols, ere ours could charge them . . . To say the truth they stood our first charge of pistols and swords, better than the rebels have ever yet done since their first beating at Worcester: especially those of the right wing – for their left gave it over sooner: for that the Prince with his life guard with sword and pistol charging them home upon the flank put them in route at the first encounter . . .'

The parliamentarian cavalry soon learnt its lesson and carried out one of the most remarkable cavalry actions of the wars at Langport in 1645. The parliamentary army was faced with the problem of attacking a very strong royalist position. The royalists were on a ridge separated from the parliamentarians by a valley with a stream in the bottom. The only way across the stream was a ford with a lane running though enclosures up to the royalist position. The enclosures were held by royalist musketeers. The lane opened into a plateau where Lord George Goring was positioned with the royalist horse. Sir Thomas Fairfax, commanding the parliamentarian New Model Army, first ordered his musketeers to clear the enclosures, which done he ordered Major Bethell to charge with six troops of horse, all formerly part of Cromwell's 'Ironsides'. The best account of what happened is probably that of Lt. Col. John Lilburne preserved in the Thomason Tracts.

> 'Bethell upon command given, led his own troop through the water, which was deep and dirty, and very narrow, the enemy having a large body at the top of the lane many times over his numbers, charged them with as much gallantry as ever I saw in my life, forcing them with the sword to give ground; which made way for Capt Evanson's troop to draw out of the lane and front with him, driving the enemy's great body and their reserve up the hill; but a very fresh body of the enemy's horse coming upon them forced them to retreat to Capt Grove who was their reserve, who drawing his men close received the enemy with much bravery and resolution, and gave liberty to his friends to rally and front with him, who all three charged the enemy's numerous bodies very furiously, and routed them quite; which made way for our musketeers to run up the hedges and gall the enemy, and for Major Desborough to draw his three troops out of the lane and front with Bethell. Upon which six troops divers mighty bodies of the enemy's came, and having disputed it soundly with their swords, the foot marching up furiously, and the other troops careered, and took away the enemy's courage and away they run. Of which charge of Major Bethell's, I heard the General, Lieutenant-General, and all the chief officers that saw it say, it was one of the bravest that ever their eyes beheld'.

CUIRASSIER ARMOUR

The composition of cuirassier armour is best illustrated by J Bingham, *Tactics of Aelian*, (Figure 3) and although it predates the civil wars by twenty-six years the component parts of a cuirassier armour did not change during that time.

Bingham illustrates a close helmet or field head-piece which is the type of helmet usually found on cuirassier armours in England. The front of the helmet pivots to allow the wearer to put it on and it is held shut by the lower swivel hook. The part of the helmet which protects the face divides into two parts, the visor, being the uppermost part, and the upper-bevor, which is the part with ventilation holes. Both can be raised clear of the face, as in Bingham's illustration, or the visor alone can be raised by means of a small peg on its right-hand side. The upper bevor is secured, when down, by a swivel hook. Another form of cuirassier's headpiece, instead of a visor and upper-bevor, has a pivoted fall, or peak, and a form of visor consisting of vertical bars. Later versions have the vertical bars fixed to the fall (Figure 6). Known to have been worn by troops from Savoy and possibly originating from there is a third type of cuirassier's helmet, a few examples of which are to be found in this country. This is the so-called Todenkopf or Savoyard. It has a visor pierced with eye, nose and mouth holes in a manner reminiscent of a skull and a fall which is arched over each of the eye-holes (Figure 5).

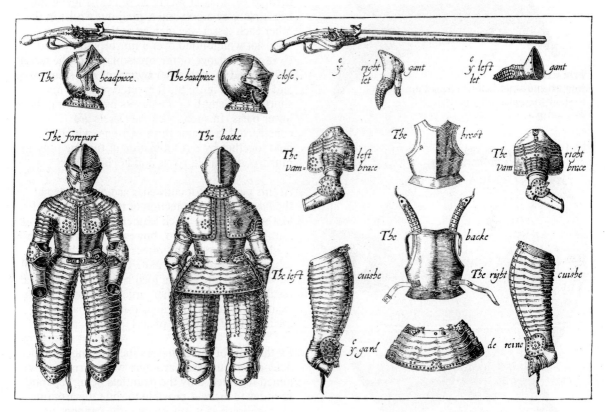

Figure 3
Cuirassier Armour from J Bingham, Tactics of Aelian, 1616. Although the armour of the cuirassier did not change by the 1640's pistols were much shorter and usually flintlocks rather than the long wheellocks shown here.

Bingham's illustration shows how the back and breastplate are attached to each other, something usually hidden by the pauldrons or shoulder-pieces on an assembled armour. The waist-straps simply buckle around the breastplate whilst the shoulder-straps, with their protective steel plates, have pierced ends which fit over pierced lugs on

11

Figure 4
English cuirassier helmet opened up
to show the constituent parts.
Royal Armouries IV 1026.

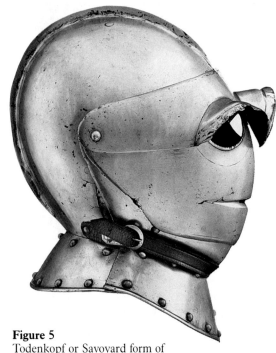

Figure 5
Todenkopf or Savoyard form of
cuirassier headpiece. This helmet is
fastened by means of a strap rather
than a swivel-hook.
Royal Armouries IV 48.

the breastplate and are held in place by swivel
hooks, in this case on the straps, which locate into
the pierced lugs. The other, narrower, straps
which in the sixteenth century would have been
fixed to the gorget, secure the arm defences to the
backplate by means of the buckles on the
pauldrons. Also clearly shown is the way in which
the tassets, which protect the legs, are attached by
hinges with removable pins to each side of the gard
de reine, or culet, which protects the lower back.
This whole arrangement rests on the wide flanges
of the back and breastplates, secured at the rear by
a hook engaging in a stud on the backplate which
passes through the culet, and at the front by a
short belt. When being worn the angle of the
backplate to the culet prevents the pins of the two
hinges from slipping out. Two other methods of
securing the tassets were in use at this time. In one
method each tasset was fixed to the flange of the
breastplate by a bolt and a wing-nut whilst in the
other each tasset was pierced at the top by a keyhole slot which fitted over a mushroom-headed
rivet on the flange of the breastplate and the tassets
were joined to each other by means of a short strap
and buckle (Figure 6). It is often possible to
shorten the length of the tassets by removing the
lower parts. In such cases the tassets are
constructed in two or three sections, which are
held together by a combination of turning pins and
mushroom-headed rivets and keyhole slots.

At this period most cuirassier armours ended at
the knee and the protection of the lower leg and
foot was left to the thick leather riding boot. A
number of armours did, however, continue to be
made with greaves, to protect the lower leg, and
sabatons, to protect the foot. These were made to
be worn over the square toed riding boot and as a
result are generally rather large and shapeless. An
example of this is the gilt armour of Charles I
made in 1612. (Colour plate 1).

By the time of the civil wars the arm and shoulder
defences of cuirassier armours were permanently
joined together, only the gauntlets being separate.
In order to make it possible to slide the arm into
the vambrace as it was known, the cannon, or
forearm defence, was made in two parts hinged
longitudinally at the back and closed by a simple
pin catch which depends on the natural spring in
the steel plates. The gauntlets are finely articulated
pieces of armour with flaring cuffs, usually pointed
and with thumb defences joined on by a small
hinge.

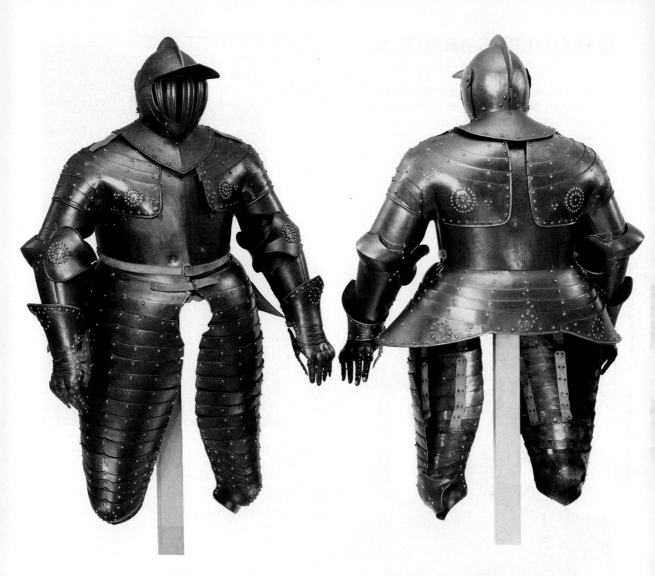

Figure 6
This very large cuirassier armour is
German dating from the 1630s. It
shows one way of attaching tassets by
means of keyhole slots.
Royal Armouries II 198.

Figure 7
This view of the same cuirassier
armour shows how a separate culet
could be attached. It also reveals the
joins in the tassets as well as the way
they are articulated.
Royal Armouries II 198.

HARQUEBUS ARMOUR

By the mid-seventeenth century, the armour of the harquebusier had been reduced until it comprised only back, breast, helmet (Figure 8) and, occasionally, an elbow-gauntlet for the left forearm and hand. Originally the armour included a gorget, but the need for this was obviated when the harquebusier lost it's shoulder defences. In the sixteenth century these were attached to the gorget, and, instead, the neck lines of the back and breastplates were raised to compensate for the loss of the protection.

Figure 9 (Above)
Harquebus armour shoulder strap and fastening. This example from the Littlecote House armoury still has its original leather.
Royal Armouries III 1969 and 2007.

Figure 8 (Left)
Harquebus armour consisting of back, breast and three-barred pott. Many armours of this type were made during the 1640's and 1650's and cost about 20s each.
Royal Armouries II 231.

The waistline of the armour is high, both for comfort on horseback and in line with the high waist of civilian fashion. The breastplate has a strong medial ridge and a narrow flange, which is continued on the backplate. Frequently a circular dent can be seen on the breastplate where it has been 'proved' against pistol or carbine shot. This means that a test shot has been fired at the armour to 'prove' that it is shot-proof. If the shot made a hole or crack the armour was destroyed. The back and breastplates are held together by straps at the waist and shoulders. The waist-belt does not go all the way around the armour, but is riveted to the sides of the backplate and fastens, with a simple buckle, around the breastplate. Riveted to each shoulder of the backplate is a leather strap covered with a series of small iron plates and with a long, slightly curved plate, usually pierced by two keyhole slots, riveted to the end of it. On each side of the breastplate is a mushroom-headed rivet, which fits into the keyhole slots to hold the armour together at the shoulders.

Over the years the leather straps on these armours have rotted and been replaced, but at Littlecote House one was found which still retained its original leather straps. This revealed that the plates on the straps were riveted to the leather in a single long strip, only partly cut through, and were subsequently broken into separate pieces. This resulted in the closest possible fit between the plates giving very good protection to the leather straps against sword cuts. It is also a particularly

easy and efficient way of attaching the plates (Figure 9).

The flange around the bottom of the back and breastplate is narrower than that on either a cuirassier's or pikeman's armour because it does not have to support tassets or a culet.

Most harquebus back and breastplates are stamped at the neck with the mark or initials of the maker. The mark of the Armourers Company of London is also often found. This was originally a letter A surmounted by a crown, but was replaced with a letter A surmounted by a helmet in 1650. From about the same time many harquebus armours were also marked with the cross of St George which formed part of the Commonwealth Arms introduced in 1649.

The helmet usually associated with English harquebus armours was known during this period

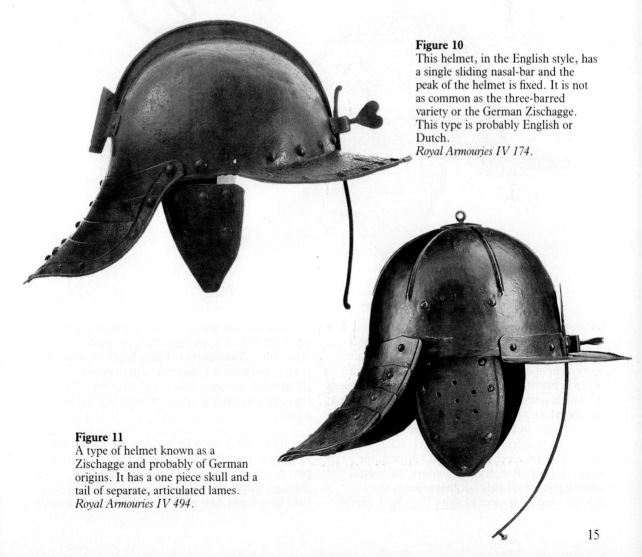

Figure 10
This helmet, in the English style, has a single sliding nasal-bar and the peak of the helmet is fixed. It is not as common as the three-barred variety or the German Zischagge. This type is probably English or Dutch.
Royal Armouries IV 174.

Figure 11
A type of helmet known as a Zischagge and probably of German origins. It has a one piece skull and a tail of separate, articulated lames.
Royal Armouries IV 494.

15

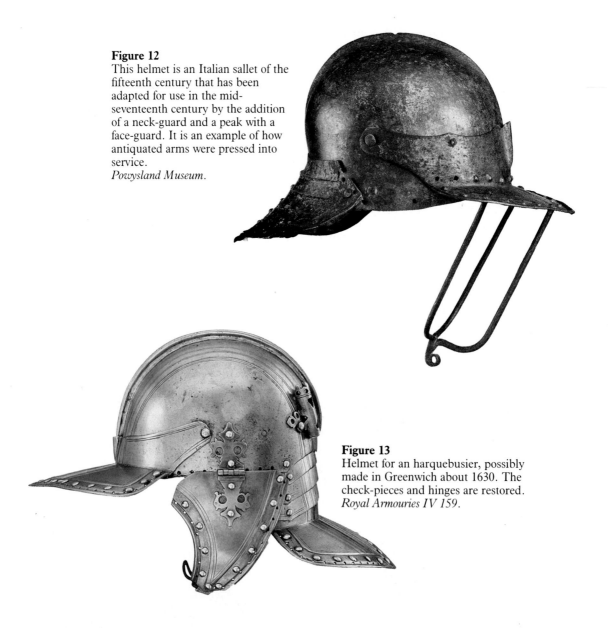

Figure 12
This helmet is an Italian sallet of the fifteenth century that has been adapted for use in the mid-seventeenth century by the addition of a neck-guard and a peak with a face-guard. It is an example of how antiquated arms were pressed into service.
Powysland Museum.

Figure 13
Helmet for an harquebusier, possibly made in Greenwich about 1630. The check-pieces and hinges are restored.
Royal Armouries IV 159.

as the three-barred pott and now as the lobster pott. It is a peculiarly English design of helmet and consists of a skull formed in two halves, the joint forming a raised comb, a tail or neck-guard, and a pivoted peak with a face-guard of three bars. The neck-guard is usually formed as a single piece decorated with simulated lames. It is the similarity between this and the tail of a lobster that gives the helmet its modern name. On better-quality helmets, particularly on German helmets, the neck-guard is often made up of separate lames resulting in an articulation that mimics the lobster's tail even more closely. The cheek-pieces

of these helmets are generally of one piece, but again some better-quality examples have articulated cheek-pieces. These helmets, made as part of a complete harquebus armour, were stamped in the same way as the back and breastplates, usually on the peak or the neck-guard.

Another helmet worn by harquebusiers was the Zischagge from which the English three-barred pott derived (Figure 11). It has a fixed peak through which slides a single nasal-bar. This is held by a screw fixing on the front of the helmet.

ROYAL ARMOURIES MUSEUM

GUNMAKERS AT THE ROYAL ARMOURIES

REGISTERED
GUNMAKER

Expert Gunmaking, Restoring and Firearms Engraving

Jack Truscott and Stephen Gledhill, two of Britains most experienced craftsmen in the field of antique and vintage firearms restoration are pleased to announce the opening of a traditional gunmakers workshop.

Over 60 Years Experience

Backed by considerable expertise and years acquiring specialist knowledge, Jack and Stephen endeavour to make their workshop a centre of excellence as gunmakers in the fields of firearm manufacture, restoration and decoration.

No Commission Too Challenging

Based at the Royal Armouries Museum, they are able to use as reference, an almost inexhaustive range of original antique and modern weapons, ranging from the common to the obscure.

Manufacture of Weapons of Competition Quality

John Emmerson, of the GB Muzzle Loading team, uses a Japanese Matchlock pistol, hand built in the workshop, in international competition. All productions are of the highest quality.

Comprehensive Range of Service

All facets of gunmaking and restoration are
undertaken ;
Springs are a speciality – main, frizzen,
sear, etc, etc.
Wheel, Flint and Percussion Locks
Barrel blueing and browning
Choke alterations
Action tightening and jointing
Stock finishing and chequering
Antique and modern reproduction revolvers
rebuilt, retimed and regulated
Fine chiselling and engraving – all styles
Gold and precious metal inlay work

Independent Business at the
Royal Armouries Museum

Placed alongside the Royal Armouries Museum
in Leeds, The Craft Court, within which Jack
and Stephen operate, showcases traditional skills
and crafts and provides an authentic environment
for its craftsmen to ply their trades. It is from this
base that the gunmakers accept commissions for
the composition of complete weapons and the
manufacture of replacement parts, in doing so
undergoing the meticulous work required to
meet the high standards and expectations of the
modern gun enthusiast.

Gunmakers at The Royal Armouries
The Craft Court, Royal Armouries Museum,
Armouries Drive, Leeds LS10 1LT, United Kingdom.
Tel: (0113) 2548763 and (0113) 2201808
Fax: 0113 2201871
e-mail:mastergunmaker@armouries.org.uk

Many of the surviving examples originated in the Low Countries. They have a one-piece, fluted skull with a carrying ring on top. Unlike the English helmets these usually have neck-guards made up of separate lames. Many of them have unidentified *L* or *M* marks stamped on the nasal-bar and the relatively large numbers in this country suggests that they were imported just before or during the civil wars.

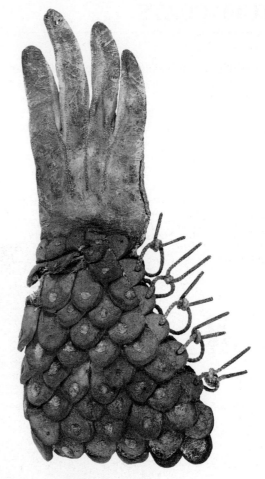

Figure 14
An example of the long elbow-gauntlets sometimes worn with harquebus armour to protect the left hand and arm.
Royal Armouries III 1476.

Figure 15
A gauntlet made of overlapping scales of buff-leather.
Royal Armouries III 822.

The final piece of an harquebus armour is the elbow-gauntlet (Figure 14). This was made for the left arm to protect the bridle hand and extended right up to the elbow. The fingers and hand are protected by articulated plates fixed onto a leather gauntlet and the whole sleeve is lined. Little is known about the manufacture or dating of these as no marked examples are known. Although they were in use at the beginning of the wars they seem to have fallen quickly into disuse and contracts for harquebus armours make no mention of them after the early 1640s. Not all of these gauntlets were made of steel and some buff-leather examples survive with elaborate sleeves of overlapping scalloped sections (Figure 15).

BUFF-COATS

The Buff coat was widely recommended for wear under armour. Portraits suggest this was a fairly common practice. It would also appear that the buff-coat was often worn by choice as an alternative to armour. At the assault of Shelford House, in 1645,

We have already seen that cavalry from London wore either a buff-coat or armour, and indeed the wearing of buff-coats seems to have been something of a trade-mark of troops from London. An account of the battle of Newbury recorded by

Figure 16
One of the collection of buff-coats preserved at Littlecote House.
Royal Armouries III 1942.

Figure 17
A close-up of the stitching on a buff-coat showing the characteristic ridge caused by the method of sewing.
Royal Armouries III 1942.

Rushworth includes '. . . *two hundred Arms gathered up, with great store of good pillage, trained Band Buff, (for many were Londoners) . . .*'

Buff-coats were very expensive, which might explain why they appear to have been the prerogative of officers and the better off members of London's trained bands. In 1640 John Tubervill wrote to his father-in-law John Willoughby,

> *'For your buff-coat I have looked after, and the price: they are exceedingly dear, not a good one to be gotten under £10, a very poor one for five or six pounds.'*

In 1662 Captain John Hodgson complained that his buff-coat was taken away from him by a royalist official, *'I would not have taken ten pounds for it.'*

The reason for this expense becomes clear when one examines the workship that went into the making of a buff-coat. Firstly, the extreme thickness of the buff-leather requires a special kind of stitching. All the joints are butt-joints with two threads passing in opposite directions through the same holes – in through the top of the join and out through the side. When pulled tight this produces the puckered join that is characteristic of all buff-coats (Figure 17). The join on the inside is then closed with a simple running stitch. Also most buff-coats appear to have been lined with a coarse linen or sometimes silk. Some were lined completely, many only from the waist up including the sleeves. Furthermore, it is common for the edges of coats to have a linen tape along the inside where they are not lined. Many coats, particularly those in portraits, but a few extant examples as well, appear to be fastened down the front by gold or silver lacing. This would have made putting on a buff-coat a most laborious task if it was indeed the case. In fact it is likely that most of these lacings were merely decorative and simply spiralled down each side through the lace holes. The actual method of fastening buff-coats, almost without exception, as far as can be ascertained, was

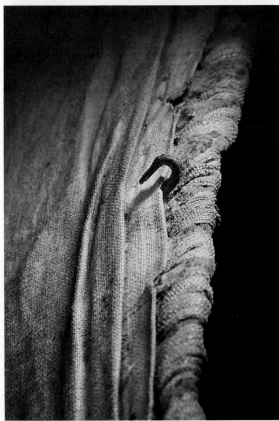

Figure 18
The inside of a buff-coat from Littlecote House showing the lining and a hook for fastening the coat.
Royal Armouries III 1942.

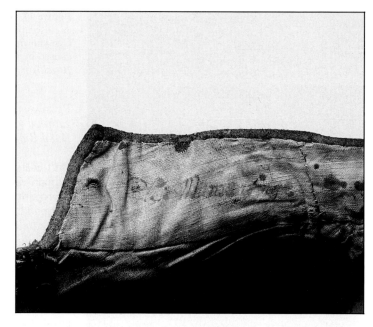

Figure 19
The collar of a buff-coat from
Littlecote House with a name written
on the lining, presumably that of its
wearer.
Royal Armouries III 1942.

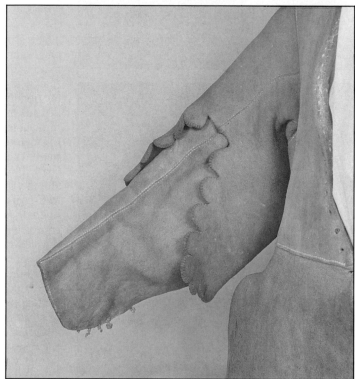

Figure 20
A buff-coat sleeve with a short thick
upper-section and a full length
thinner sleeve.
National Army Museum.

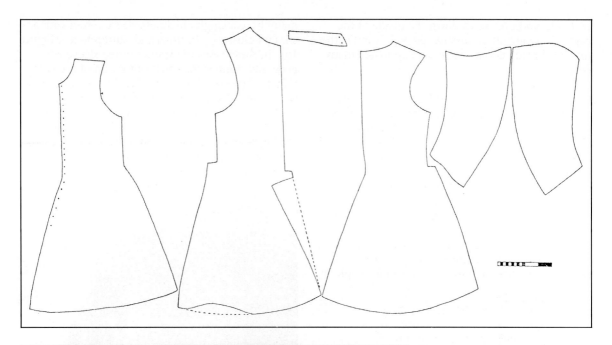

Figure 21
A pattern taken from a buff-coat
at Littlecote House.

Figure 22
A buff-coat traditionally that of the
parliamentarian Major Saunders.
National Army Museum.

by hooks and eyes sewn down the inside of the coat. These are often missing today, but indicative tufts of thread and rust spots remain inside many coats.

Of the coats in the Littlecote House collection, now the property of the Royal Armouries, all save one have lost their hooks and eyes (Figure 18), but close examination has revealed that is how they all fastened. The high collars, however, that survive on some buff-coats are all fastened by buttons and loops. These collars too are lined and one example at Littlecote still bears a name, possibly Mainwaring, presumably that of its wearer (Figure 19). Although some sleeveless buff-coats survive and some are shown in portraits, most are sleeved. Like the Littlecote examples, except that traditionally attributed to Col. Alexander Popham

Figure 23
The buff-coat of the regicide Colonel Hacker. This coat has been altered at some time by having a new row of lacing holes punched in the right-hand side.
Royal Armouries III 1301.

many have a single thickness sleeve, often with a slit cuff closed by buttons and button holes (Figure 16). In these cases the leather of the sleeve is generally thinner than that of the rest of the coat. Others, however, have a double thickness sleeve with a thin sleeve all the way from the shoulder to the wrist, and a thicker outer sleeve from shoulder to elbow. This outersleeve is usually scooped on the inside of the elbow to aid movement although sometimes the ends of the scoop are closed by a string or thong (Figure 20).

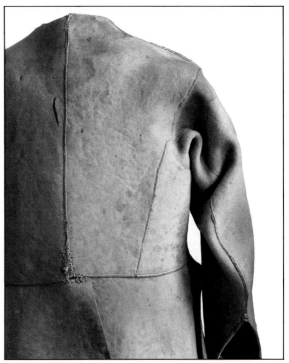

Figure 24
Colonel Hacker's buff-coat showing its construction and the cut of the panels.
Royal Armouries III 1301.

Variation is also found in the cut of buff-coats. Most of those at Littlecote have simple bodies of four pieces of buff leather (Figure 21). Others have the skirts of the coats cut as separate pieces, whilst the bodies of some are of four of even six sections, such as the buff-coat traditionally that of the regicide Francis Hacker, now preserved in the Royal Armouries (Figures 23 and 24). Another coat in the Royal Armouries has one very wide panel at the front of the skirt which fastens all the way across the front rather like an apron (Figure 26).

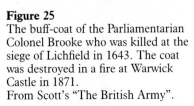

Figure 25
The buff-coat of the Parliamentarian
Colonel Brooke who was killed at the
siege of Lichfield in 1643. The coat
was destroyed in a fire at Warwick
Castle in 1871.
From Scott's "The British Army".

Figure 26
A buff-coat with an apron-like front
panel.
Royal Armouries III 1446.

One of the finest contemporary illustrations of a
buff-coat is in the portrait of Nathaniel Fiennes.
The coat has double thickness sleeves and the
right-hand sleeve illustrates clearly the scoop out
of the leather at the elbow, closed with thonging,
and the scalloped edge of the sleeve. The left outer
sleeve, however, whilst scalloped, appears to be
much shorter and to finish above the elbow,
presumably to accommodate the long elbow
gauntlet (Colour plate 2).

SWORDS

Although firearms were important, the sword was the principal weapon of the cavalry of the English Civil Wars and was also used by all other types of soldier. Surviving records make it clear that there were different patterns for horse and foot, at least among swords supplied to the government. A contract made in 1645 with the London Cutlers Company for 3200 swords and belts at five shillings each, specifies that 200 are to be horsemen's swords. It is, however, impossible to match any contracts with existing swords and tell which are meant for horse and which for foot, if indeed there were such marked differences in practice. Similarly many contemporary writers refer to a type of sword known as a Tuck. It has not been possible, however, to identify this type amongst surviving swords. For this reason all sword types will be dealt with in this section.

Reference has already been made in the introduction to the Hounslow sword factory and although it was closed down early on during the civil wars it had been in operation since 1632 and had produces many thousands of swords and sword blades. The result is that many English swords of the period of the civil wars have blades marked Hounsloe, Hounslo, Hunsloe or other variations of Hounslow. The principal figure at Hounslow was Benjamin Stone who seems to have been the organiser of production and with whom many contracts were placed by the Office of the Ordnance. In fact he eventually became *'His Majesty's blademaker for the office of the Ordnance'* in 1636. However, many other names of bladesmiths are known in connection with Hounslow and these also often appear on swordblades. A number of these men were recruited from Germany and so the names of Johannes Hoppie and Johannes Kinndt are found along with that of the Londoner Joseph Jenckes. It was presumably Kinndt that Sir William Waller and Sir Arthur Hasselrig were referring to when in 1643 they requested *'two hundred swords of Kennets making at Hounslow'*.

The Mortuary-Sword

The modern term 'Mortuary-Sword' is now applied to a particular type of broadsword of the mid-seventeenth century that is peculiar to Britain (Figure 27). These swords have a hilt, usually of

Figure 27
A typical mortuary-sword with characteristic decoration and arrangement of guards.
Royal Armouries IX 2205.

24

Figure 28
An ornate mortuary-sword with typical chiselled and pierced decoration, including portrait busts of Charles I and Henrietta Maria.
Royal Armouries IX 2146.

Figure 29
The decoration of this mortuary-sword includes the figure of a soldier in boots and pikeman's armour and armed with a pike.
Royal Armouries IX 1214.

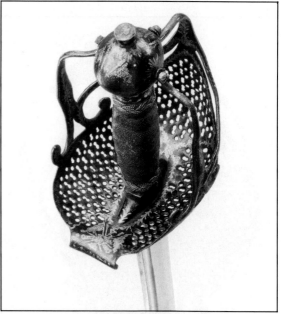

Figure 30
This mortuary-sword is decorated with an unidentified coat of arms.
Royal Armouries IX 957.

Figure 31
This is traditionally the sword carried by Oliver Cromwell at the taking of Drogheda in 1649.
Royal Armouries IX 1096.

iron, the main features of which are a dish- or boat-shaped guard or stool with a wide wrist guard, one central knuckle guard and two side knuckle-guards: each of these is linked to the central knuckle-guard by one, two, or three scroll-guards. The knuckle-guards are each screwed to the pommel. These swords usually also have a block at the end of the grip nearer the blade, from which two, usually shield-shaped, langets pass through the stool on either side of the blade. The other wide-spread, but not universal, feature of mortuary-swords is the decoration of the hilts. Many have chiselled heads of a typical 17th-century appearance, with long hair and Van Dyke beards. It is these that have given the swords their name. Egerton Castle in his *Schools and Masters of Fence*, published in London in 1885, wrote *'Swords of this type are often called "mortuary" as a number of them were made in memory of Charles I and bear his likeness upon the hilt'*.

Although one mortuary-sword in the collection of HM Queen at Windsor bears a likeness of Charles I and Henrietta Maria, as do two in the Royal Armouries there is no contemporary evidence to support Castle's statement. In fact in many cases the presence of a likeness of Henrietta Maria as well as that of Charles I would suggest that the idea is unlikely.

Other forms of decoration are also found, such as armed figures, coats of arms (Figure 30) and piercing. One sword preserved in the Royal Armouries (Figure 31) is a typical mortuary-sword but is pierced with a simple geometric pattern. It also retains much of its original painted decoration, black japanning with gold trophies of arms and foliate decoration. Traditionally this is the sword carried by Oliver Cromwell at Drogheda in 1649.

Figure 32
A very simply decorated mortuary-sword but still typical of the type.
Royal Armouries IX 1245.

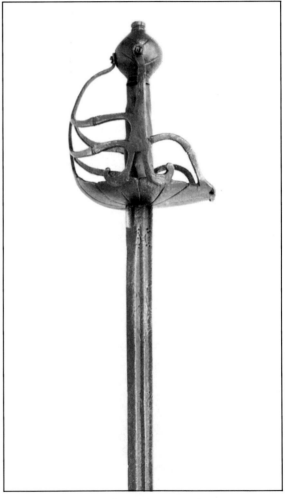

Figure 33
Another characteristic form of decoration of mortuary-swords is this use of chiselled heads and dolphins.
York Castle Museum.

Figure 34
This variation of the mortuary-sword
has scroll-guards which link the
knuckle-guard to the stool rather
than the side knuckle-guard to which
they are linked by a continuation of
the upper scroll-guards. This
example also has side bars linking the
wrist-guard to the side knuckle-
guards.
Private Collection.

Figure 35
This very fine mortuary-sword has a
blade decorated with the arms of the
Commonwealth, the date 1650 and
the words FOR THE COMMON-
WEALTH OF ENGLAND.
*Philadelphia Museum of Art: Bequest
of Carl Otto Kretschmar von
Kienbusch.*

The Proto-Mortuary Sword

This type of broad sword (Figure 36) owes its modern name to the fact that it is generally thought to be the forerunner to the mortuary sword. This, however, remains to be proven and they were certainly in use simultaneously. The hilt of the proto-mortuary sword is distinguished by having two shell-guards on either side of the hilt, usually formed from a single iron plate and often separated from each other by piercings around the blade, and a circular or shell-shaped swelling or plate in the centre of the knuckle-guard. The shell-guards are also often different sizes with the outer shell (as you hold the sword in your hand point forward) being larger. The outer shell is almost invariably linked to the pommel by a side knuckle-guard, while this feature is sometimes absent from the inner shell. Usually the swelling on the knuckle-guard is linked to both or just the outside shell-guards by one or more scroll guards. These scroll-guards often join the knuckle-guards at the swelling. The proto-mortuary sword also has a fully formed rear quillon, often formed from a continuation, right through the hilt, of the knuckle-guard and there is no langet-block. The decoration of these swords is usually simply chiselled lines and punched marks with cusped edges imitating cockle-shells. Some, however, are more ornately chiselled with heads and foliate designs like mortuary swords. The pommels of proto-mortuary swords are the same as those found on mortuary swords but there is one variation where the pommel takes the form of a stylised lion's head, the neck forming a substantial portion of the grip (Figure 38). These are almost always of cast brass and are often silver plated.

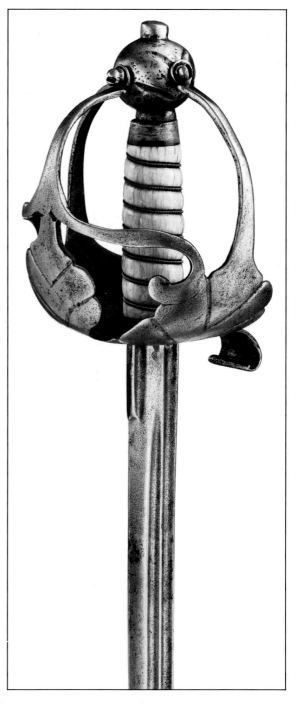

Figure 36
This is a typical proto-mortuary-sword showing clearly the distinctive swelling in the knuckle-guard and the two shell-guards.
Royal Armouries IX 1388.

Figure 37
This proto-mortuary is highly
decorated with gold scroll-work but
still retains all the basic
characteristics.
British Museum.

Figure 38
This proto-mortuary is an example of
a variant which has a lions-head
pommel. Such pommels are also
occasionally found on Mortuary
swords.
Private Collection.

The Basket-Hilted Sword

The basket-hilt had already been around for some time by the mid-seventeenth century. It developed in Britain during the sixteenth century and was often referred to by contemporary writers as the Irish Hilt. At that time, the term 'Irish' was applied to the Gaelic speaking inhabitants of both Ireland and Scotland. The hilt of a basket-hilted sword is primarily made up of three sets of three bars each. The bars of each set meet at the pommel to form a tongue which is generally screwed to the pommel. Where the outside bars of a set touch a bar from another set they form a saltire-like feature and this junction is often formed into a disc or plate. Emerging from the central of the nine bars and passing on either side of the blade are two loop-shaped guards. The pommels of this type of sword are usually large and spherical although a few munition quality basket-hilts have flat bun-shaped pommels. Amongst the finer swords the ends of the sets of bars are screwed to the pommel, although with munition examplesoften only the central group is screwed to the pommel. The finer examples tend to have wide flat bars usually decorated with encrusted silver designs (Figure 39) whilst munition quality swords have much thinner bars sometimes of almost circular section.

Figure 39
English basket-hilted sword. The ribbon-like bars are decorated with silver inlaid foliage patterns.
Royal Armouries IX 1114.

Figure 41
This basket-hilted sword, since
stolen, was excavated on the site of
Basing House which was destroyed in
1645.
Photograph C. Blair.

Figure 40
Munition quality basket-hilted sword
with crude punched decoration. The
blade is marked 1648 but that may
not be the date of manufacture.
Royal Armouries IX 223.

The Hanger

The term hanger is generally applied to any short sword, usually with a curved blade, and the mid-seventeenth century in Britain saw a type that is of an indigenous design (Figure 42). It usually has two shell guards, the outer one, being larger and curved towards the point and the inner one, sometimes absent, smaller and curved towards the pommel. The grip, sometimes made of wood with wire binding, sometimes of stag or buck-horn, has a ferrule with a flat top and prominent tang button and a scrolled extension to which the knuckle-guard is screwed. The knuckle-guard invariably has a decorative feature at its mid-point and runs through the hilt to form a rear quillion, which often has a terminal echoing the decorative feature of the knuckle-guard. The blades of these hangers are curved and often have a falchion-type point with a false edge on the back of the blade, others have pierced or saw-backed blades. Decoration varies on these swords both in style and quality, but most common is a dot and trellis pattern in silver (Figure 42).

Figure 42
A fine example of an English hanger with a pierced blade.
Royal Armouries IX 755.

Figure 43
An English hanger with a variation of
the usual form of decoration.
Royal Armouries IX 942.

Figure 44
This hanger has a grip made of stag-
horn.
Royal Armouries IX 1390.

The Rapier

In Britain, during the second quarter of the seventeenth century, the rapier developed into a number of closely related types, which were peculiarly British.

The earliest type, dating from 1625-1640, has a hilt consisting of a cup, through the centre of which passes the blade, surmounted by two or three circular guards all linked by struts and with a pair of quillons, straight or recurved, and a knuckle-guard. The pommel is frequently ovoid with fluting or ribbing (Figure 45). Similar to this type is a variant which instead of a cup, through the centre of which passes the blade, has two plates shaped like cockle-shells (Figure 46). Another common form (Figure 47) also has a cup around the blade, which is almost invariably decorated in relief, whilst in the first type (Figure 45) the cup is usually pierced. Also the cup is frequently asymetrical. The relief decoration on the cups of this type of rapier often uses portraits of Charles I and Henrietta Maria as on mortuary swords.

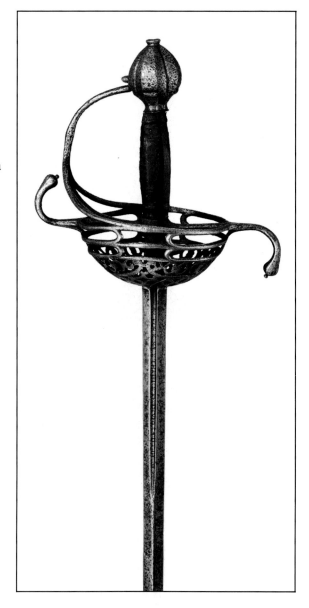

Figure 45
A typically English rapier with a pierced cup surmounted by rings and with recurved quillons. The blade is inscribed FOR MY CHRIST RESOLVED TO DIE.
Royal Armouries IX 1380.

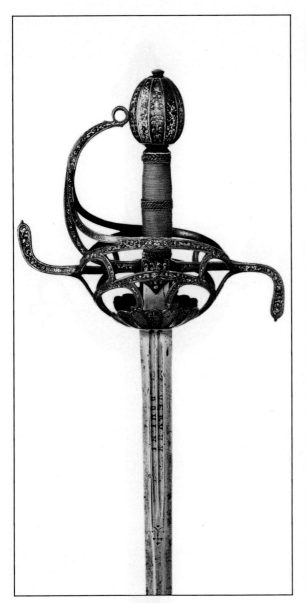

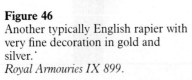

Figure 46
Another typically English rapier with
very fine decoration in gold and
silver.
Royal Armouries IX 899.

Figure 47
This rapier is decorated with
chiselled heads of Charles I and
Henrietta Maria against a fire-gilt
ground.
Royal Armouries IX 883.

Figure 48
The steel hilt of this rapier is
chiselled with fleur-de-lys and the
Prince of Wales feathers.
Royal Armouries IX 956.

Figure 49
This rapier is decorated in a style
resembling that found on mortuary-
swords and generally considered to
be English.
Royal Armouries IX 982.

Pattern Swords

Although it has not been possible to relate them to any documentary evidence some designs of swords from the mid-seventeenth century occur in such numbers that they can be considered as regulation pattern swords. The first of these is of typical mortuary sword form (Figure 50). It has a shallow stool and wide wrist-guard, one central and two side knuckle-guards and one or, more usually, two scroll-guards. Occasionally, the wrist guard is linked to the side knuckle-guards by side bars. However, apart from the consistency of their form it is the unvarying decoration of the stool that marks them out as a pattern. On either side of the blade is chiselled a crude square head and the rest of the stool is taken up by crudely chiselled stylised foliate decoration. Although there is inevitably some variation in detail from sword to sword due to the individual chisellers the basic pattern is remarkably consistent.

The second type is a crude proto-mortuary sword (Figure 51). The hilt has two shell-guards both curved towards the pommel, the outer shell being larger and having a side knuckle-guard. The knuckle-guard passes through the hilt to form a rear quillon and has a central swelling from which a scroll-guard links it to the right shell. The grip is cylindrical and the pommel is a flat circular cap. The decoration is limited to simple crude chiselled lines. One example in the Royal Armouries (Figure 52) has a blade marked on each side *FOR THE TOWER*.

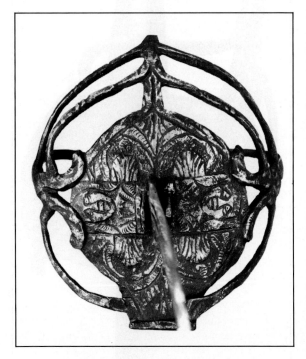

Figure 50
This shows the decoration common to the 'pattern' mortuary-sword.
Royal Armouries IX 2127.

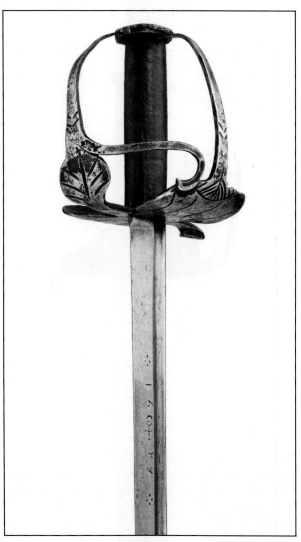

Figure 51
The construction of the hilt of this sword can clearly be seen as can the chiselled decoration common to all the swords of this type.
Royal Armouries IX 216.

The third pattern sword (Figure 53) has a hilt consisting of a shallow, almost oval, stool, a knuckle-guard which is screwed to the pommel and at the other end joins a bar which forms the recurved front and rear quillons and widens around the tang to form a block supporting langets on either side of the blade (Figure 54). The knuckle-guard is linked to the stool on both sides by scroll-guards. The long pommel is like that found on some English rapiers of this period. The decoration is of very crude chiselled lines and resembles that on the pattern proto-mortuary.

Figure 52
Another example of the 'pattern' proto-mortuary this one has a blade marked FOR THE TOWER.
Royal Armouries IX 206.

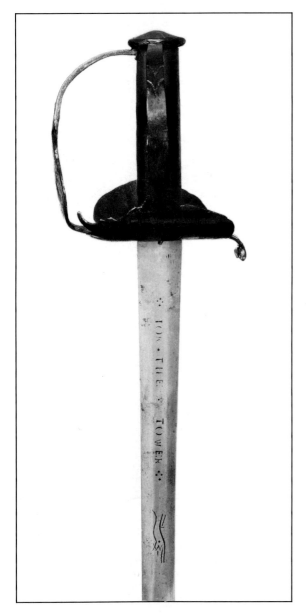

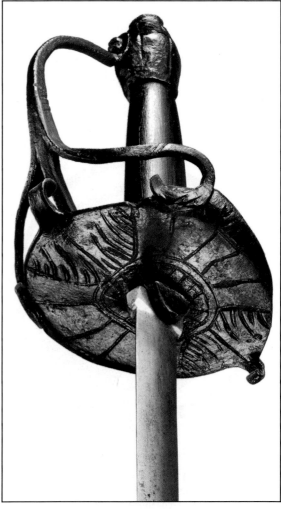

Figure 53
The decoration on this sword is common to all of this type and is similar to that in figure 52.
Royal Armouries IX 217.

A fourth pattern sword is another proto-mortuary (Figure 55) but of a better quality than the previous one (Figure 51). Its general form is typical of the proto-mortuary. It has two symmetrical shell-guards. These shells are in turn joined to the pommel by side knuckle-guards. It is, however, the decoration as much as the form of the hilt that characterises this pattern. In addition to lines and cusped edges the centre of both shell guards is decorated with a grotesque bearded face, possibly leonine, a motif which is repeated on the knuckle-guard swelling.

Figure 54 (below Left)
Another view of the same sword showing the construction details. *Royal Armouries IX 217.*

Figure 55
This sword is of classic proto-mortuary sword form. The crudely chiselled decoration, a leonine face and radiating lines, are common to this 'pattern'. *Gunnersbury Park Museum.*

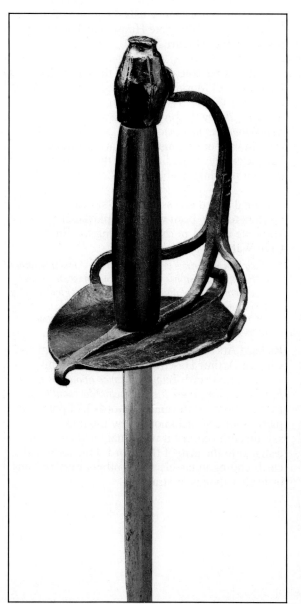

Accessories

Every sword, of course, had its scabbard. At this time they usually consisted of a wooden lining covered with leather, although sometimes they were covered with cloth. In order to prevent the scabbard from slipping out of its belt or hanger a long hook was fixed to the outer face of the scabbard. This protruded through the leather covering whilst the inner end was fixed by a binding of fine twine (Figure 57). Metal fittings, or lockets, around the mouths of scabbards did not appear until the middle of the century and then only as a narrow binding around the scabbard mouth. It was not until the 1660s that the locket became large enough for the hook to be mounted on it.

At the time of the English Civil Wars two forms of sword belt were in use, the waist-belt and hanger, and the baldrick. The waist belt was frequently fastened by means of a simple central catch whilst the adjustment of the belt was by a buckle that was to the right-hand side of the wearer. On the belt were two rings mounted on slides, one worn at the right hip and one on the left to which was fastened by means of hooks the long strap which passed across the front of the body and was known as the side-piece and the part which carried the sword and was known as the hanger. The hanger itself was a broad leather sling which was divided into two or three straps which were again divided into two, three or even more loops closed by slides (Figure 58). The side-piece attached to the hanger at its lower front corner or ran through the loops to the rear.

A variation of this sword belt is a top mount with a hook to fasten to the belt, with a number of straps with what amounts to small hangers of two or three loops each buckled to them. A similar variation is to be found with baldricks (Figure 57).

The baldrick, or shoulder sword belt, was generally fastened with a buckle at the front but some illustrated in portraits have no apparent join. Those at Littlecote are certainly made that way. Some although fastened with buckles are richly embroidered in relief and in paintings are almost always shown still fastened when laid aside. Another variation is in Dobson's painting of an unknown officer where the baldrick is fastened by two laces (Colour plate 3). The lower end of the back of the baldrick divides into loops with slides and, like a hanger, is sometimes split into two straps, each terminating in a number of loops. Often the rear group of loops were left hanging unused. As with the waist-hanger a variation exists where groups of loops are fastened to straps by buckles (Figure 57). By the mid-seventeenth century, however, the rear end of the baldrick particularly on military examples was simply divided into two large loops without buckles or slides. Into this category falls the group of baldricks from Littlecote House which are simply sewn together (Figure 59).

An interesting note on wearing the baldrick comes from Frances Markham writing in *Five Decades of Epistles of Warre*, *'The Bautrick gerdle (being loose) is apt to fall (by the poyze of the Sword) in a troublesome manner before him . . .'*. This could explain why often waist sashes are worn over baldricks; they would tie down the sword and prevent it swinging about.

The final sword accessory is the sword-knot which appears to have been widely employed at this time. JB wrote in 1661 of cavalry during the English Civil Wars:

> *'their Encounterings being not after the Antient Manner of Firing at a distance and Wheeling off (which hath been found to be of dangerous Consequence) but to fire at a neere Distance, (their Swords hanging at their wrists by a string) and with their Swords points charging through adverse Troopes . . .'*

Richard Atkyns at the end of his running fight with Sir Arthur Haselrig bid him give up his sword. The sword *'being tied twice about his wrist, he was fumbling a great while before he would part with it.'* Some 16th century swords had pommels pierced for a sword knot but by the mid-seventeenth century it was usual for them to be fastened to the grip of the sword. One form had cords ending in tassels whilst others were ribbons or leather thongs or straps.

Figure 56
Captain Jacob Symonz de Vries in
1633, wearing a very fine baldrick.
Amsterdam Historisches Museum.

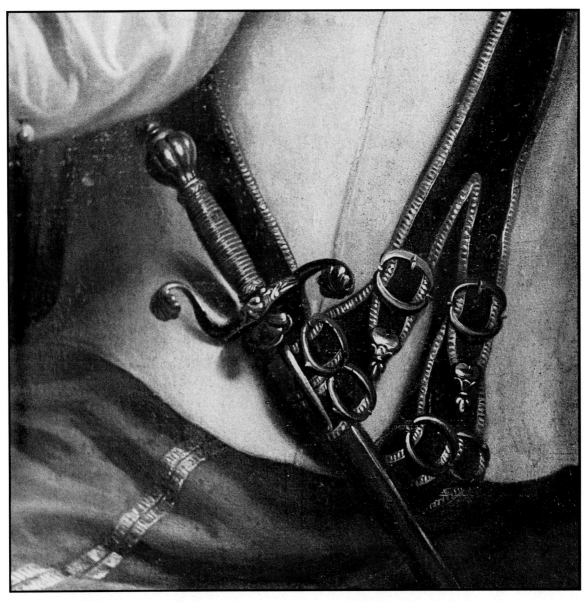

Figure 57
A detail of the Dutch painting of the
Company of Captain Jan Symonsz
Jongemaets by J A Rotias, dated
1655.
Westfries Museum, Hoorn.

Figure 58
A finely decorated hanger with twelve loops.
Royal Armouries IX 1409.

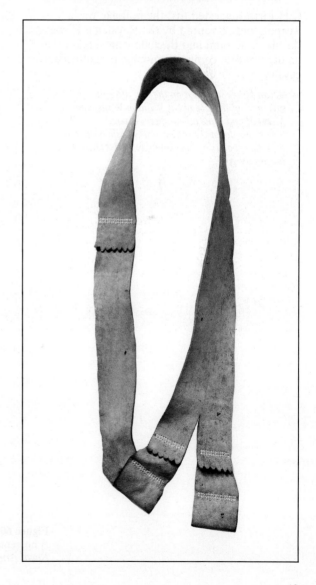

Figure 59
A baldrick of buff-leather from Littlecote House.
Royal Armouries IX 3356.

Pollaxes

In addition to swords, cavalry often carried another cutting weapon, the pollaxe. In his description of the arming of the Harquebusier Vernon wrote that he should have *'a good poll axe in his hand'* (Figure 60). He continues

> *'A poll axe is very necessary for a trooper, for if you should encounter a troop of Cuirassiers where your sword can do no good but little execution, your poll axe may be an advantage unto you to offend your enemie'.*

At the battle of Edgehill the royalist Sir Richard Bulstrode was

> *'wounded in the head by a person who turned upon me and struck me with his pole-axe, and was seconding his blow, when Sir Thomas Byron being near, he shot him dead with his pistol . . .'.*

C H Firth suggested that the poll-axe was a weapon more favoured by the Royalists. However, the above account and the following suggest that its use was also common amongst parliamentarian cavalry.

> *'Dean Ryves says that on the day after the surrender of the city to Sir William Waller the Marshal and some other officers entered . . . As they broke down the organs and smashed the pipes with their pollaxes they scoffingly said "Hark how the organs goe".'*

Figure 60
A horseman's pollaxe.
Royal Armouries VIII 106.

CAVALRY FIREARMS

The descriptions above of how a trooper should be equipped and the accounts of various cavalry engagements have already shown the wide extent to which the cavalry employed firearms. Three classes of firearm were in use, pistols, carbines and blunderbusses and there were two main types of lock providing ignition, the wheellock and the flintlock. The use of the wheellock in Britain was never as widespread as it was on the continent although the royalists appear to have imported large numbers from the continent. For example a letter from a royalist agent in Holland contains a reference to *'10 Chists Containing 500 Paire of pistolls, with the spannars'* being shipped from Amsterdam (Figure 61). What actually tells us that the pistols were wheellocks is the term 'spanner' which refers to the tool used to wind up the mechanism of the wheellock (Figure 62). Indeed one problem of identifying a particular type of lock in contemporary documents is that the term firelock was used indiscriminately to describe both wheellocks and flintlocks. (For a description of the

different locks and an explanation of terminology see the appendix).

The Parliamentarian forces on the other hand seem to have mainly used flintlock firearms, although in April 1645 Major Harrison of Fleetwood's Regiment took delivery of 120 pairs of pistols with holsters and spanners. There was good reason for this preference. The wheellock was an intricate ignition system by comparison to the flintlock and very apt to go wrong, with potentially fatal consequences. Vernon wrote *'never span (wind up) before you have need, because many times the firelock pistols will not go off, if they have stood long spanned'*. Sir Edmund Ludlow had personal experience of this problem at the siege of Wardour Castle. A Royalist mine had blown a breech in the wall of his room and, cut off from his men, he had to defend the breech alone and with only his sword, *'My pistols being wheellocks and wound up all night, I could not get to fire'*. Not only were flintlocks more reliable than wheellocks but they were also cheaper. The statutory rates of pay for gunmakers laid down in 1631 specified £3 for a pair of wheellocks and £2 for a pair of flintlocks.

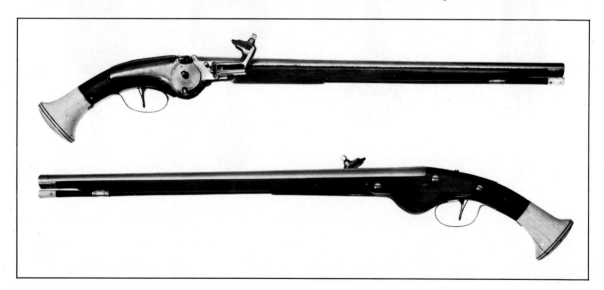

Figure 61
Dutch wheellock pistols
with ivory butt-caps.
Royal Armouries XII 1267-8.

Figure 62
A group of spanners for winding-up
wheellock firearms. Three have built
in priming-flasks.
Royal Armouries XIII 46, 45, 44, 47.

Pistols

The primary firearm of the cavalry was the pistol, invariably carried in pairs, with one pistol in a holster hanging on each side of the front of the saddle. Indeed amongst the forces of Parliament they were usually the only firearm carried by the cavalry. An order of the Council of War in 1630 specified that pistols should have 18 in. barrels, be 26 in. long overall and have a bore of 24 bullets to the pound *'rowleing in'*. By the time of the civil wars the average barrel length appears to have been reduced to 14 in. or 15 in. This was discovered when the Civil War firearms at Littlecote House, which now form part of the collection of the Royal Armouries, were catalogued for the first time in 1984. Study of this collection also revealed a wide variation of lock mechanisms, lock shapes, and even materials used, one group having brass lockplates.

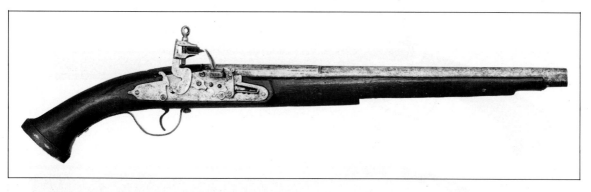

Figure 63
A typical English-lock pistol of the civil wars. This example has a damaged fore-end and the ram-rod is missing.
Royal Armouries XII 1681.

Figure 64
Three pistols from Littlecote House made by the London gunsmith Robert Murden.
Royal Armouries XII 5438, 5414, 5437.

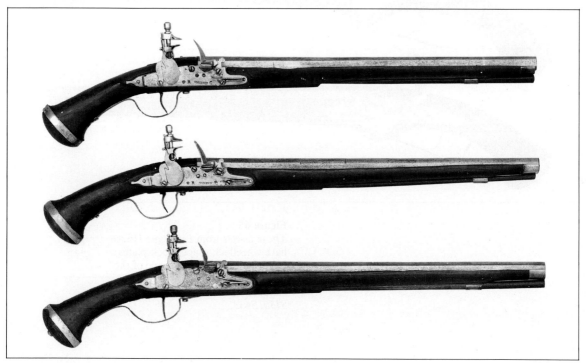

Generally speaking, whether wheellock or flintlock, pistols of this period have long slender stocks with gently curved butts terminating with a flared butt end to give a good grip (Figures 61 and 63). The wheellock in addition has a bulge in the stock in front of the trigger-guard to house its wheel. This feature is also sometimes found on flintlocks, with the lock-plate cut to match, but serves no practical purpose at all (Figure 65). Most English pistols of this period use a type of lock, known as the English lock, which was peculiar to this country. On pistols, and carbines, it is generally fitted with a dog-catch, a simple swivelling hook which catches on the tail of the cock. Barrels on English pistols are quite often octagonal for their whole length but round barrels and barrels which change from octagonal to round are also common.

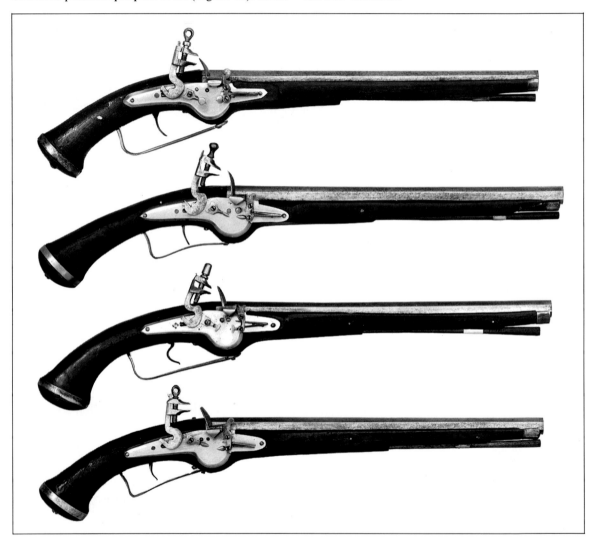

Figure 65
These pistols from Littlecote House have wheellock shaped lock-plates but are flintlocks. The shape of the plates serves no purpose at all.
Royal Armouries XII 5431, 5432, 5430, 5433.

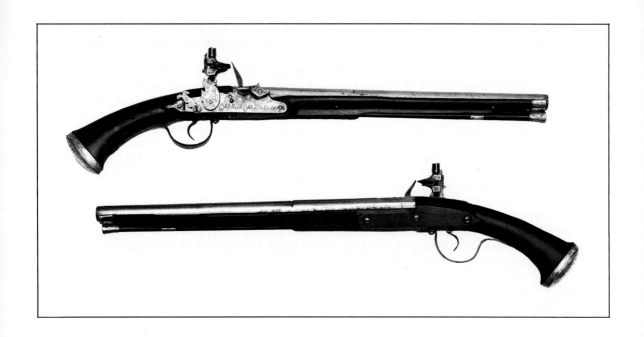

Figure 66 and 67
This pair of pistols by the London gunsmith William Watson have the arms of the Commonwealth on their barrels.
Royal Armouries XII 1495-6.

The accounts of cavalry engagements given above have already shown how the pistol was considered to be very much a weapon for use at close quarters. Ludlow even reported that at Marston Moor

> *'The horse on both sides behaved themselves with the utmost bravery; for having discharged their pistols, and flung them at each others heads, they fell to it with their swords'.*

Another common ploy was to double shot pistols. In 1645 during the relief of Taunton, by troops under the command of Colonel Ralph Weldon, a parliamentarian cavalry officer was engaged in combat with a cornet of Sir Ralph Hopton's Lifeguard. The cornet attempted to escape, *'but he was soon overtaken by his Pistoll, which ended his journey by a brace of bullets in his back . . .'.*

Carbines

The use of carbines was not as universal as that of pistols. On the parliamentarian side the cavalry of the Earl of Essex appear to have used carbines but amongst others, and in particular Fairfax's New Model Army, their use was not widespread. Only after 1649 when the army's duties were more of a policing nature was the cavalry generally armed with carbines. Before then their use seems to have been largely restricted to officers. In early 1649 a leader of the Levellers' mutiny called Thompson, was shot dead by a corporal who had borrowed his colonel's carbine. Amongst the royalist cavalry the use of carbines seems to have been more widespread. The surviving records for the royalist army at Oxford show large numbers being issued but often, it would appear, as an alternative to pistols. When Colonel Blagge was raising a troop of one hundred cuirassiers in 1644 he was issued with sixty pairs of pistols and forty carbines.

The same order of the Council of War in 1630 that specified the dimensions of pistols also dealt with carbines. Like the pistol, the carbine was to be 24 bore but with a barrel length of 30 in. and an overall length of 45 in. During the civil wars, however, a barrel length of 2 ft or 2ft. 6 in. seems to have been usual. In 1639 the price of a carbine was £1 16s 0d for a wheellock and £1 2s 0d for a flintlock. During the war itself Parliament was buying flintlock carbines in London at 12s 9d, whilst carbines imported from Holland were costing the royalists £1 11s 0d each (Figure 68). Similarly Parliament was paying between 18s for a pair of pistols in 1646, compared to £1 6s 0d or £1 8s 0d in 1645, while royalists were paying as much as £2 11s 0d for a pair imported from Holland.

Figure 68
A Dutch wheellock carbine probably very like the ones imported by the royalists.
Royal Armouries XII 61.

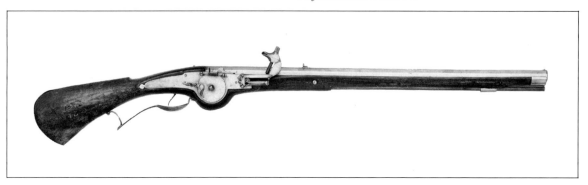

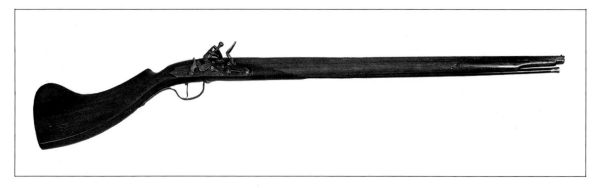

Figure 69
An English-lock carbine.
Hampshire County Museum Service.

Blunderbusses

When the Leveller leader Thompson was shot in 1649 it was recorded that the carbine used *'being charged with 7 bullets gave Thompson his death's wound'*. It is possible, however, that the weapon used was not a carbine as such, but a blunderbuss. Sir James Turner in *Pallas Armata*, (London 1683) wrote of harquebusiers *'Some instead of Carabines carry Blunderbusses, which are short Hand-guns of a great bore, wherein they may put several Pistol or Carabine-Balls, or small Slugs of Iron'*. In 1677 the Earl of Orrery, a veteran of the Irish wars, wrote in *A Treatise of the Art of War: 'And if in the Front of our Squadrons we had some Blunderbushes, they might be of good use in Fight'*. The extent to which Blunderbusses were used during the civil wars is not clear. However, 265 were repaired for the Board of Ordnance in 1654 suggesting that they had been in use for some time. Blunderbusses are recorded in Holland from the 16th century, the earliest known example being a matchlock in the Westfries Museum, Hoorn, which dates from about 1575. Furthermore it seems probable that the co-called Littlecote carbines are in fact blunderbusses. Their bores are all of 0.82 in., with the exception of two of 0.84 in., larger not only than carbine bore but musket bore as well (Figure 70). It has been suggested that the Littlecote guns,

thirteen in all, may be examples of the type of gun known as a dragon. In January 1645 a contract was placed for the supply of *'Two hundred snaphaunce Dragoones full bore & proofe at 12s 4d a peece'*. Markham, however, wrote in his *Souldiers Accidence, 'these Dragons are short peeces of 16 inches, the Barrell, and full Musquet bore . . .'* He was describing a firearm for use by *'Dragons, which are a kind of footmen on horsebacke'*. Since during the civil war dragoons were armed mainly with flintlock muskets, it is possible that the term 'dragon' had come to mean any short barrelled, large bore, cavalry firearm but was soon replaced by the term blunderbuss.

Unfortunately, the Littlecote blunderbusses lack any marks or other indications of nationality. A private collection in America, however, contains a blunderbuss similar to the Littlecote guns, by a known English gunmaker. The lock of this gun is inscribed *W Phippes* (Figure 71). William Phippes is known to have been making guns in London between 1645 and 1661. Indeed, a member of the Blacksmiths Company, he became a victim of the struggle between the Blacksmiths and the emerging Gunmakers Company for control of the gun making trade: he was arrested in 1658 for making firearms whilst not a member of the Gunmakers' Company.

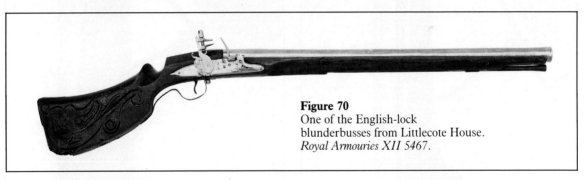

Figure 70
One of the English-lock blunderbusses from Littlecote House.
Royal Armouries XII 5467.

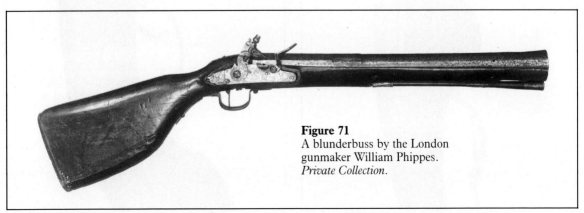

Figure 71
A blunderbuss by the London gunmaker William Phippes.
Private Collection.

Carbine Belts

Carbines, blunderbusses and dragons were all carried by cavalry in the same way, suspended from a belt worn diagonally over the left shoulder so that the gun hung by the wearer's right side ready for use. On the belt was an iron fitting with a spring-clip which fastened onto a loose ring on the gun. This ring could be attached to the gun in two ways: either through a hole in a screw-head, or sliding along a steel-bar fixed to the side of the gun (Figures 72 and 73).

Figure 72 (Left)
This shows a carbine belt attached by means of a bar and sliding-ring. *Royal Armouries XII 61 and XIII 304.*

Figure 73 (Right)
A carbine belt with a carbine attached by a simple ring in the side of the carbine. *Royal Armouries XII 5480 and XIII 303.*

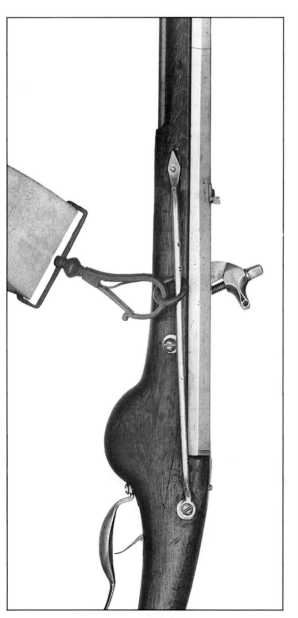

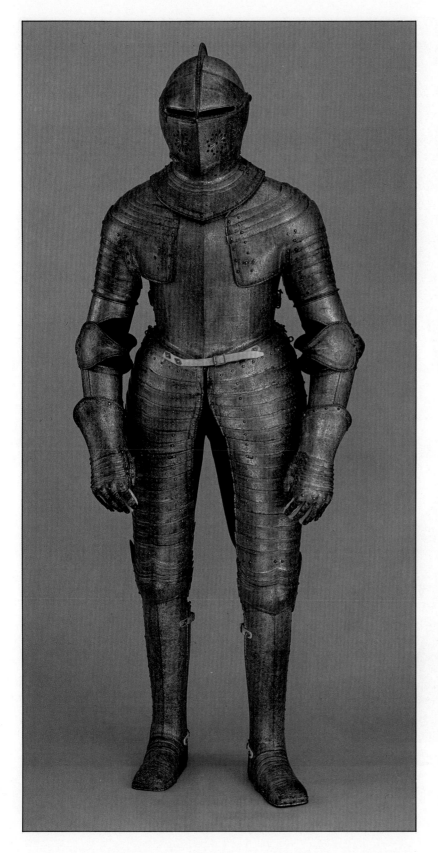

Plate 1
The gilt armour of Charles I,
Dutch, about 1612
Royal Armouries II 91.

THE HON.^{BLE} COLONEL
NATHANIEL FINES.
MIREVELT. PINX.^T

Plate 2
Portrait of the parliamentarian
Nathaniel Fiennes
Courtesy of Lord Saye and Sele

Plate 3
An unknown officer by Dobson
Courtesy of Lord Sackville

Plate 4
Portrait of Col. Thomas St Aubyn
Pencarrow House, Bodmin.

Plate 5
Equestrian portrait of
Col. Alexander Popham
Royal Armouries I 315.

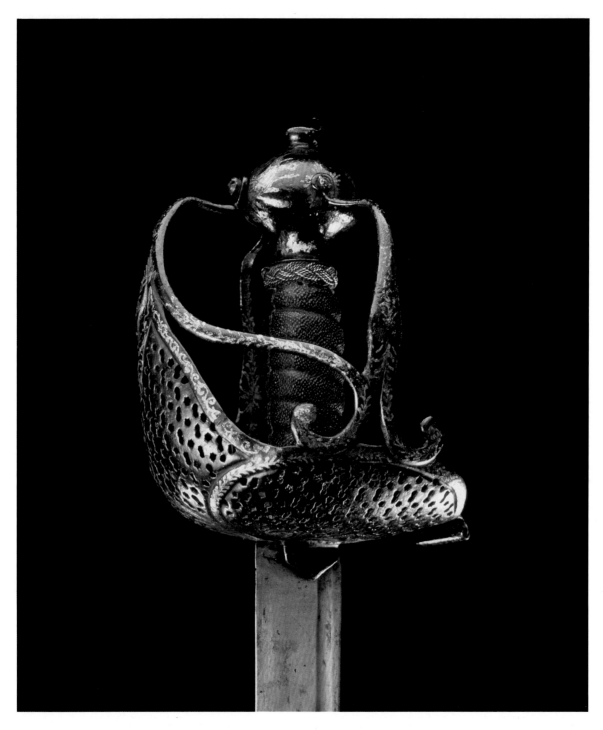

Plate 6
Oliver Cromwell's mortuary sword
Royal Armouries IX 1096.

Plate 7
An artillery piece in action in a field-
battle. By the French artist Pieter
Meulener (1602-1654).
Royal Armouries I. 330

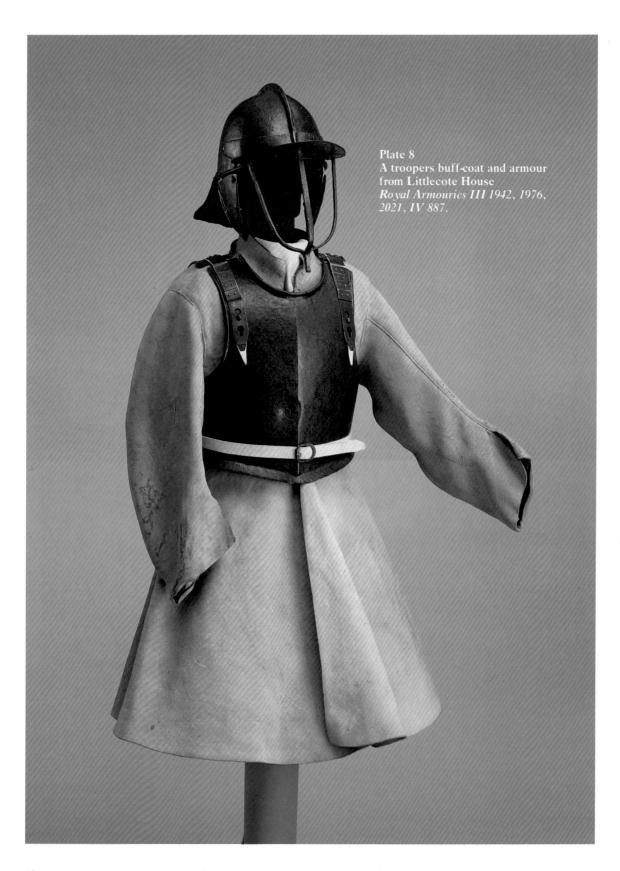

Plate 8
A troopers buff-coat and armour
from Littlecote House
Royal Armouries III 1942, 1976,
2021, IV 887.

The INFANTRY

There were two types of infantryman employed during the English Civil Wars, the pikeman and the musketeer. Of these the musketeer was the more numerous, generally outnumbering the pikeman by about two to one. It was also upon the musketeer, with his long range weapon, that the bulk of the fighting fell; whereas the pikeman, whose effectiveness was limited to the length of his pike, either confined his activities to defending the musketeer against cavalry, or was used to push home any advantage to try and achieve a decision in the outcome of a fight (Figure 74).

This division of labour is clearly presented in the Duke of York's account of the battle of Edgehill in

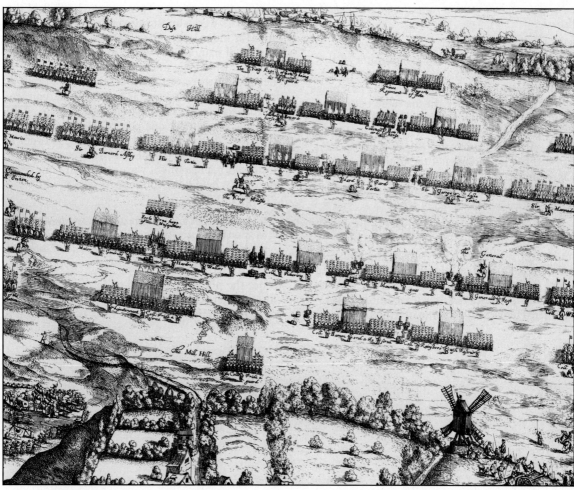

Figure 74
This illustration, from Sprigge's
Anglia Rediviva shows how civil war
infantry formed-up with the pikemen
in the middle flanked by musketeers.

1642. He describes how the royalist forces advanced on the waiting 'rebels', both sides firing until some regiments were at push of pike. On this occasion, however, the pikes failed to achieve a decision and

'each as if by mutual consent retired some few paces, and then struck down their colours, continuing to fire at each other even till night . . .'.

The Duke found this outcome *"very extraordinary"* as once regiments had come to push of pike one side or the other usually broke and ran. Certainly that is what happened at Naseby. There the royalist foot broke the first line of the parliamentarian army only to be broken in turn by the second line. Cromwell describing the battle of Dunbar wrote *'my own regiment . . . at the push of pike, did repel the stoutest regiment the enemy had there . . .'.*

The pikeman's other task was to counter the cavalry. Perhaps the best known example of this was the stand made by the Whitecoats at Marston Moor in 1644. They, however, had the advantage of being in an enclosure. In the same battle, the regiments of Lindsay and Maitland, who were in the open, used their pikemen to drive back Lucas's horse. At Newbury, Prince Rupert's horses were stopped by the pikemen of the trained bands. Clarendon says of the royalist cavalry that they *'endured their storm of small shot'*, but *'could make no impression on their stand of pikes.'*

Neither was the musketeer helpless in the face of cavalry. For close quarters work the English musketeer was in the habit of using his musket as a club, taking hold of it by the barrel and laying about him with the butt end. The Duke of York at the Battle of Dunes nearly fell victim in that manner. He had led a charge of exiled royalist cavalry, fighting for the Spanish, against the English infantry, who were fighting with the French. They broke into the infantry who continued to resist the cavalry *'so that we ran as great a danger by the butt end of their musketts as by the volley they had given us'*. The butt end of the musket was also employed against other infantry. At Naseby Sir Edward Walker described how the infantry of the two sides clashed, the royalists *'falling in with Sword and butt end of the musquet.'* Also at Naseby, one royalist brigade stood against cavalry until Fairfax's own regiment of infantry *'fell in with them, with Butt-end of Muskets and so broke them.'*

The musket of this period was not a particularly accurate weapon and was only effective when employed in numbers. Thus, on the battlefield the musketeers were almost invariably drawn up in six ranks, as indeed were the pikemen. For firing, a number of manoeuvres were employed, some quite complex. Either the musketeers fired by ranks, one, two, or three at a time, or a number of ranks or files were marched forward clear of the regiment in order to fire and then marched back again. The principle was to have one part of the musketeers firing, one ready to fire and one loading in order to keep up a continual hail of shot. However, when closing with an enemy it was usual to fire one or two volleys before the musketeers fell on with clubbed muskets.

'I gave the order to the first three rancks to discharge at once; and after them the other three; which done we fell pell mell into their ranks, knocking them down with the stock of the musket and our swords'.

Hence the phrase often used to describe infantry in close quarters combat; *'at push of pike and with butt end of musket.'*

PIKEMAN'S ARMOUR

The military manuals of this period are unanimous in saying that the pikeman should wear armour. However, none of them suggest that a pikeman should wear a buff-coat and there is no evidence to suggest that any pikeman did, with the possible exception of members of the London Trained Bands. The elements that make up a pikeman's armour are a helmet, gorget, backplate, breastplate and tassets (Figure 75).

During the period of the civil wars the wearing of pikeman's armour declined and there is no evidence for the manufacture of it in this country after the early 1640s. It is difficult to assess the rate at which it fell into disuse. There is no doubt that the Earl of Essex's infantry was well supplied with armour (Figure 76), much of it imported from Holland in 1642 and 1643 (Figure 77), but this was lost when the infantry surrendered at Lostwithiel and it does not seem to have been replaced. On the other hand the King's infantry at the battle of Edgehill is described by Clarendon, '. . . in the whole body there was not one pikeman had a corslet . . .'. The New Model Army, formed

in 1645, certainly had no pikeman's armour issued to it but that does not mean it was not in use. As the New Model Army was made up of elements from other armies some infantry may have brought armour with them. In 1658, however, Lockhart who commanded the English troops in Flanders wrote requesting *'twelve or fifteen hundred corslets for our pikemen'*. He subsequently received at least five hundred from the Tower.

It has been suggested that the abandonment of armour during this period was a gradual development, with gorgets and tassets going first. Monck, who was writing in 1645, recommends as the defensive arms of a pikeman, *'An Head-piece with Back and Breast; a Buff Girdle of double Buff*

Figure 75
Pikeman's armour from J Bingham, Tactics of Aelian, 1616. Clearly visible are the methods of attaching the tassets and fastening the shoulder straps. On the waist-belt of the armour are slides for the attachment of a sword-hanger and on the flange of the backplate is a hook on which the helmet could be carried.

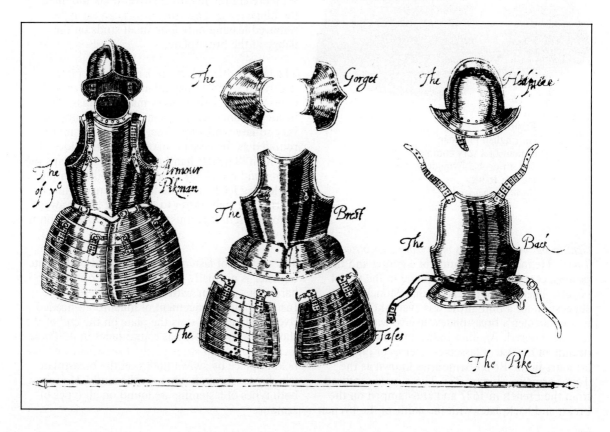

Figure 76
An English pikeman's
armour of a very common
pattern probably made in
the late 1630s.
Royal Armouries II 214.

Marshal Toiras. Instead of tassets and breastplates
have a deep flange at the waist to give some
protection. These armours aside, however, the vast
majority of surviving pikemen's armours were
abandoned as a whole rather than piece by piece.

Like the harquebus armour the breastplate of
pikemen's armour has a strong medial ridge, but
apart from this there are more differences than
similarities. The neck line of both the back and
breastplate of a pikeman's armour is cut low, a
gorget being supplied to protect the throat. The
flange at the bottom of the breastplate is deeper
than that on an harquebus armour as it has to
support the attachment of the tassets; indeed, both
because of that, and because of the similar neck
lines, it is easier to confuse a pikeman's breastplate
without tassets with a cuirassier's breastplate than
with an harquebusier's breastplate. Invariably, the
tassets are joined to the flange of the breastplate by
two hinges rivetted onto each tasset, but the
method of fixing the hinges to the flange varies.
Many are simply rivetted, making removal by the
soldier difficult. Others, however, have a slot cut
in the top of the hinge which fits over a protruding
stud on the flange. The hinge is then held in place
either by a pin passing through a hole in the stud
or, more commonly, by a swivel-hook mounted on
the hinge itself. Thus the tassets can easily be
removed leaving only four small studs on the
flange of the breastplate.

The tassets themselves are large, single plates
decorated with simulated lames and patterns of
rivets, the latter sometimes made of brass. The
inside bottom corner of a tasset is generally cut
very square whilst the outer corner is far more
rounded as the tassets curve around the sides of
the thigh. The left-hand tasset always overlaps the
right-hand one. This is because in pike fighting
the left leg leads, and the left tasset needs to
overlap the right tasset to prevent it lifting away
from the right leg, thus reducing the protection it
provides.

The method of fastening the back and breastplate
together is normally the same as that on the
harquebus armour with one main difference.
Instead of an arrangement of mushroom-headed
rivets and keyhole slots the plate on the end of the
shoulder-trap simply has round holes in it. These
locate over round studs on the breastplate and are
held in place by swivel-hooks on the breastplate
which pass through a hole in the studs. However,
both types of fastening are found on all types of
armour.

*eight inches broad which is to be worn . . . instead of
Taces'.* He makes no mention of a gorget and the
passage certainly suggests a decline in the use of
tassets. There is no indication that Monck's
suggestion for a buff girdle was ever taken up but
many pikemen's breastplates survive with their
tassets removed. Another indication of the early
decline of the use of tassets is a series of pike
armours in the Royal Armouries known as the
Toiras armours (Figure 78). These were captured
from the French in 1627 and are stamped on the
breast and backplates with the name of the French

Figure 77
A Dutch pikeman's armour probably of the type imported during the early part of the civil wars.
Royal Armouries II 165.

Figure 78
Pikeman's armour captured in 1627 from the French and bearing the name of Marshal Toiras. These armours now have English helmets which according to tradition were made to go with them.
Royal Armouries III 250.

Figure 80
A pikeman's armour with an unusual
design on the tassets. A similar
armour was stolen from the church at
Cropredy Bridge.
Royal Armouries II 118.

Figure 79
A decorated English pikeman's
armour, possibly made at Greenwich
between 1620-30.
Royal Armouries II 271.

The pikeman's helmet, or pott, as it is generally
known, is of a two-piece construction, joined like
the lobster pott at the comb, but with a brim all
the way round. It is a very simple form of helmet,
with single piece cheek-pieces and usually,
although not invariable, a plume holder,
sometimes in brass, at the back.

The final element of the pikeman's armour is the
gorget (Figure 81). It consists of two plates which
are pivoted on the left-hand side and fastened on
the right by means of a keyhole slot and
mushroom-headed stud. These are frequently very
simple and plain pieces of armour but some are
designed to be worn alone, perhaps over a buff-
coat and can be very fine pieces (Figure 82). An
example of this can be seen in the portrait of
Colonel Thomas St Aubyn dated 1641 (Colour
plate 4).

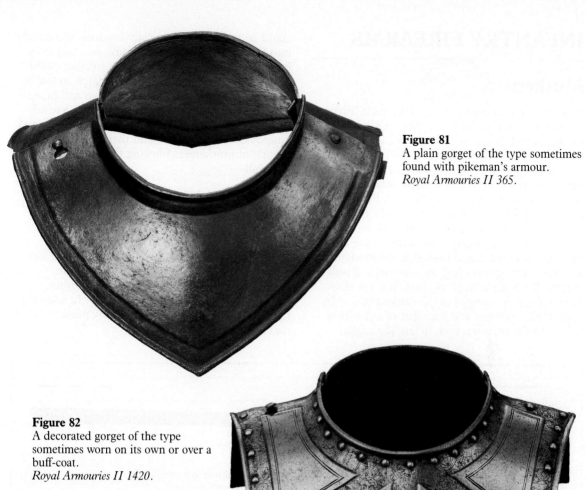

Figure 81
A plain gorget of the type sometimes
found with pikeman's armour.
Royal Armouries II 365.

Figure 82
A decorated gorget of the type
sometimes worn on its own or over a
buff-coat.
Royal Armouries II 1420.

INFANTRY FIREARMS

Muskets

Both matchlock (Figure 83) and flintlock (Figure 85) muskets were used in the English Civil Wars, the matchlock being by far the more common. It was also the cheaper, costing in 1645 from between 10/- to 11/6d compared to 14/6d to 15/6d for a flintlock. As the only difference between the two types of muskets was the type of lock fitted this differential reflects the simplicity of the matchlock as opposed to the flintlock (Figures 84 and 86). Yet the matchlock had many drawbacks. Once the flintlock was loaded and cocked it was ready to fire instantly. The shooter had only to aim and pull the trigger. With the matchlock, however, the slow burning match clamped in the serpent had to be continually adjusted and kept free of ash which might hinder ignition, and, before the trigger

could be pulled, mechanically lowering the match into the priming-pan, the priming-pan had to be manually opened. In addition the weather could wreak havoc; rain could soak the match so that it went out, or between opening the pan and firing the rain could dampen the powder, or the wind blow it away. Just having a burning match around gunpowder was a hazard and there are many reports of musketeers blowing themselves up. At Edgehill

'a careless soldier in fetching powder where a magazine was, clapped his hand carelessley into a barrel of powder with his match between his fingers, whereby much powder was blown up and many killed'.

The sheer quantity of match required for an army also presented considerable problems. The garrison of Lyme in 1644, 1,500 men strong, frequently used 5cwt. of match a day. In addition, the glow of matches could give away musketeers at night.

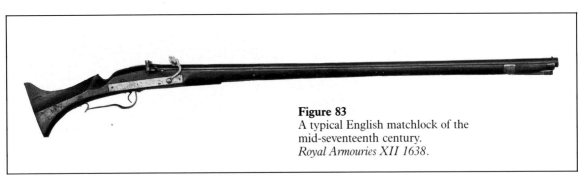

Figure 83
A typical English matchlock of the
mid-seventeenth century.
Royal Armouries XII 1638.

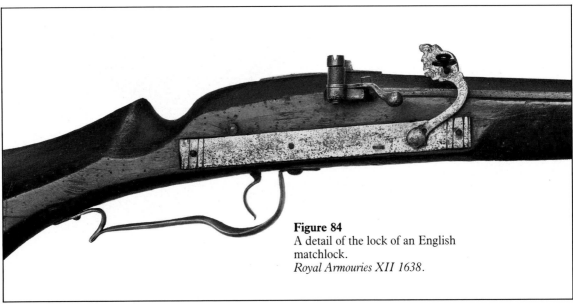

Figure 84
A detail of the lock of an English
matchlock.
Royal Armouries XII 1638.

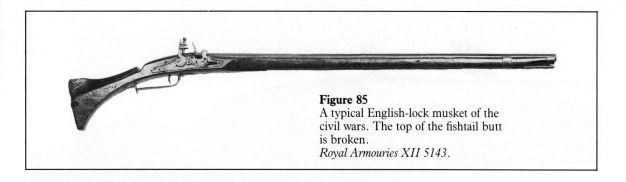

Figure 85
A typical English-lock musket of the
civil wars. The top of the fishtail butt
is broken.
Royal Armouries XII 5143.

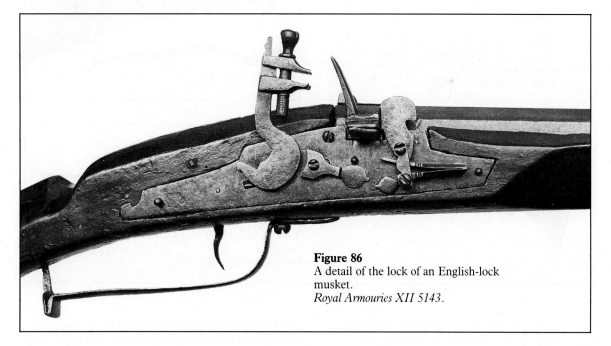

Figure 86
A detail of the lock of an English-lock
musket.
Royal Armouries XII 5143.

The usual matchlock (Figure 84) takes the form of
a long narrow plate let into the stock of the musket
inclining down at a slight angle from the axis of
the barrel from front to back. This plate which is
held by two screws from the other side of the gun
(Figure 87), conceals a very simple system of
levers and springs that move the cock to the pan
against the action of a spring when the trigger is
pulled. The screw-operated jaws of the serpent act
as a vice to hold the slow match and are often
modelled and decorated in the form of a monster's
head.

The flintlock, however, usually an English-lock
(Figure 86 and appendix), is a much more
complex device and consequently has a much
larger lockplate. Like the matchlock it is secured
at a slight angle to the barrel by screws from the
other side of the gun. The general external

appearance of the various types of flintlocks is
quite similar although internally the mechanisms
vary. It should also be noted that, unlike pistols
and carbines, flintlock muskets using English
locks are not, as a rule, fitted with dog-catches.

As for the barrel of the musket, the Council of
War in 1630 laid down that it should be 4ft. long
and of 12 bore (that is, firing balls of lead weighing
12 to the pound). In 1639, there were some
experiments with shorter barrels of 3ft. 6in., but
by the outbreak of war 4ft. had been settled on as
the standard barrel length. These barrels are
almost invariably of octagonal section at the breech
and taper towards the muzzle. About a third of the
way along they change from octagonal to round
section but, in fact, all the underside of the barrel
hidden by the stock is round, the octagonal flats
being filed on. At the breech of a matchlock,

69

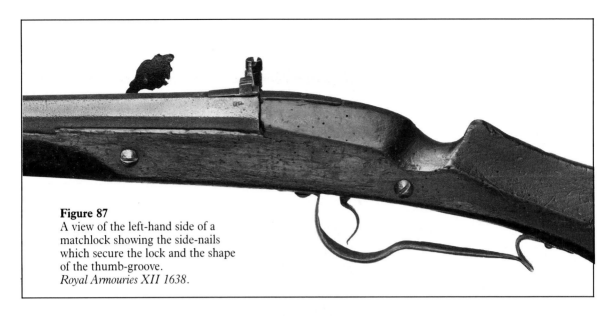

Figure 87
A view of the left-hand side of a
matchlock showing the side-nails
which secure the lock and the shape
of the thumb-groove.
Royal Armouries XII 1638.

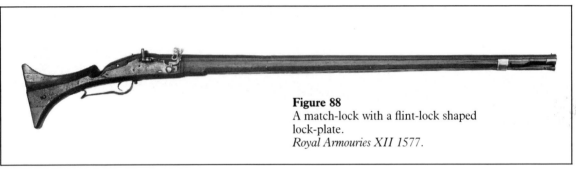

Figure 88
A match-lock with a flint-lock shaped
lock-plate.
Royal Armouries XII 1577.

beneath the touch-hole, is a shallow rectangular
recess into which is brazed the priming pan.
Flintlocks, however, have pans which are integral
to the lock. On matchlocks a shallow slot is also
filed in the breech end of the barrel on the right-
hand side to locate the flash-guard. The other end
of this is wrapped around a long screw, which
screws into the outer rear corner of the priming
pan and around which the pan cover pivots
(Figure 89). Frequently matchlock barrels are
found reused on flintlocks and in these instances
the recesses to take the pan and flash-guard have
been filled in.

The barrel is held in the stock by pins which pass
through the wood and through small pierced lugs
dove-tailed to the underside of the barrel. At the
breech a long screw passes up through the stock
from the front of the trigger guard, which it thus
secures, and into the barrel-tang. The rear of the
trigger-guard is often simply formed into.a point
and hammered into the stock.

For a munition weapon the stocks of civil war
muskets are quite long and elegant with some very
subtle shaping, particularly around the butt
(Figure 87). At the fore-end the stock is protected
by a simple metal band while a few inches away
towards the butt another strap retains the ramrod
in its groove. At the other end the rather fragile
comb of the fish-tailed butt is protected by a butt-
plate which usually only covers the top half of the
butt, sometimes additional protection is afforded
by a narrow metal strap pinned to the top of the
comb itself.

The most important surviving group of muskets
from the English Civil War period is in the Great
Hall of Littlecote House. There are eighty-two
muskets altogether, about half and half matchlock
and flintlock and many retaining their original
fish-tail stocks. One curious fact to come out of
recent study of these muskets is that while the
official barrel length of a musket of this period was
48in the barrel lengths at Littlecote range from

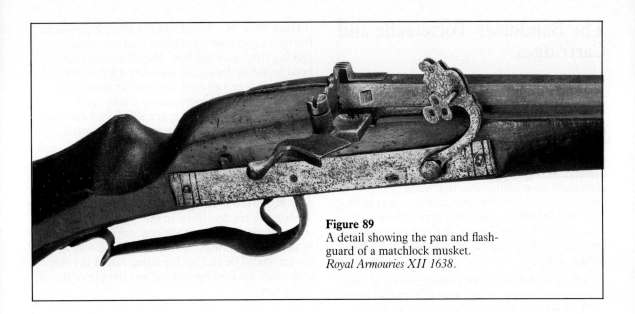

Figure 89
A detail showing the pan and flash-
guard of a matchlock musket.
Royal Armouries XII 1638.

41¾ to 47in. However, two matchlocks on loan to
the Royal Armouries from the Middle Temple do
have barrel lengths of 48in. Also at Littlecote are
sixteen barrels bearing the proof mark of the
London Gunmakers' Company introduced in
1638. Two of the muskets also bear, on the barrel,
the mark of a coronet over a combined *C L* mark.
This was introduced in 1643/4 and was to be used
on all equipment belonging to Parliament. The
C L presumably stands for Commons and Lords.
Another two muskets are stamped with the mark
of the Liège Perron. The Perron is a market cross
in the centre of Liège and was used as the town's
proofmark on firearms.These two muskets may
therefore be part of a consignment of 5,000
muskets purchased in 1640 from a Liège merchant
by the Council of War.

The Bandoleer, Portetache and Cartridges

The ammunition for a musket was generally carried in a bandoleer. This consisted of a leather belt worn over the left shoulder, from which hung a number of containers for powder and a small bag for musket balls. These powder containers have often been referred to as apostles because there are usually twelve on a bandoleer, but there is absolutely no evidence that this was a contemporary term. Records and accounts of the time usually refer to the containers as boxes or, sometimes, charges. One of the best descriptions comes from the contracts of material for the New Model Army,

> *'The boxes of the said 2000 Bandoleers to bee of wood with whole bottoms, to bee turned wthin and not Bored, the Heads to be of Wood, and to be layd in oyle (viz). Three times over, and to bee coloured blew wth blew and white strings with strong thred twist, and wth good belts, att Twenty pence a peece . . .'*

(Figure 90 & 91). Wood was the usual material for the boxes although sometimes lead was used for making the top of the box. No references have been found to these lead tops, but a large number have been found all over the country from sites such as Marston Moore, Sandal Castle, and Colchester. Wooden boxes are also found covered in leather and some are even made of tin-plate. One ornate bandoleer in the Royal Armouries, made for the guard of the Elector Christian II or John George I of Saxony in about 1605, has tinned iron plate boxes covered with velvet (Figure 92). Also preserved in the Royal Armouries are some of the bandoleers described in the New Model Army contracts (Figure 91). Each box was suspended from a pair of strings by loops in such a way that the top could be slid up the string out of the way of the box for loading without any danger of it being lost.

Figure 90
A drawing of a bandoleer and a cross-section of one of the boxes from Scott's The British Army.

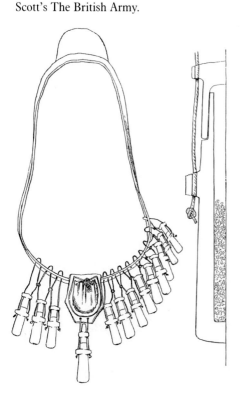

Figure 91
A bandoleer of the type used by the New Model Army.
Royal Armouries XIII 93.

At the bottom of the belt was a small leather bag closed by a draw-string, which held the musket balls. Suspended from this bag or the belt at the same point was a priming flask. This was a small flask of wood or bone which contained the powder for the priming pan of the musket. Quite frequently, however, a box was used just like the others on the bandoleer, except that it was equipped with a top with a spout for pouring out the powder.

As an alternative to the bandoleer the portetache was sometimes carried. This was a vertical leather flap on which was hooked a large powder flask, a smaller priming flask and a ball-bag. The spout of the larger flask had a cut-off at both the top and the bottom, enabling it to be used to measure the correct charge of powder. The method of using this portetache is well-illustrated by De Gheyn (Figure 93), but by the time of the civil wars they seem to have fallen into disuse.

The royalist forces of the civil wars seem to have had difficulties in obtaining sufficient bandoleers for the army. Frequent references to *'powder baggs for musketeers wth hangers for swords . . .'* suggest that they used these instead. The most likely explanation of these *'powder baggs'* is that they were used for carrying ready-made cartridges, consisting of rolls of paper containing powder and ball. In this they may, in fact, have been in advance of the parliamentarian forces which used bandoleers. Orrery is very adamant that cartridges are preferable to bandoleers. He says that bandoleers are very noisy because their boxes clatter together, giving warning of surprise attacks and preventing orders from being heard. He further complains that they can catch fire easily, killing the musketeer, and also that they can easily become tangled. Another danger must have been that the wood of the boxes would swell thus jamming the tops on, and this may explain the use of lead tops. Far better would be cartridges carried

Figure 92
A bandoleer with boxes made of tin-plate covered in velvet.
Royal Armouries XIII 91.

Figure 93
An illustration from de Gheyn's Wappenhandlung showing a portetache in use.

73

in cartridge boxes. Orrery says that as these would be worn on a belt under the soldier's coat they would be kept dry. In addition, with ball and powder being together, they could both be rammed home in one go with the paper of the cartridge acting as a wad whereas with a separate ball wadding was often omitted causing inaccuracies and sometimes even allowing the ball to roll out before firing. He further says that the cartridge boxes should be of tin as used by the cavalry. A contract dated 10 January 1645/6 does detail *'1200 Cartridges the boxes of strong plate covered wth black leather'* and these may well have been for use by the cavalry rather than the infantry.

Figure 94
An illustration from Wallhausen's Kreigskunst zu Fuss showing a bandoleer a worm and a scourer for cleaning a musket.

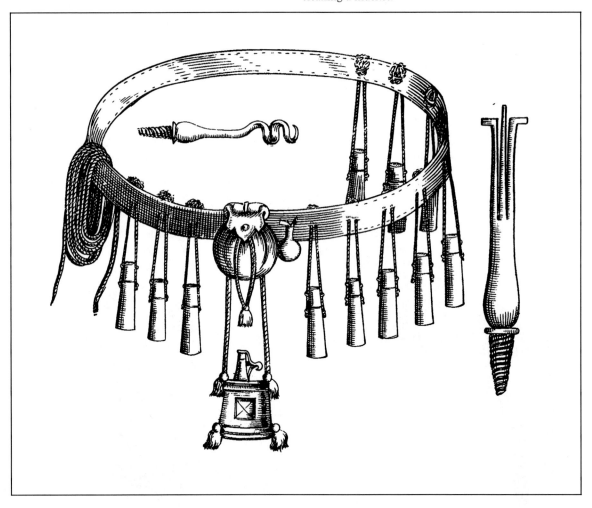

74

STAFF WEAPONS

The Pike

The principal weapon of the pikeman was of course the pike. As a general rule the length of a pike seems to have been 16 feet, as in a contract placed on 22 December 1645 with John Edwards for *'five hundred Pikes of good Ash sixteen foote long wth steel heads at three shillings xd a pike'*. The surviving royalist records include a receipt for pike staves which are only 15 feet long. It seems unlikely however that royalist pikes were as a rule shorter than parliamentarian ones as such a thing would be of considerable conseqence and hardly likely to go unreported. Such a difference in length had had a decisive influence at the battle of Benburb in Ireland in 1646. There the Irish under Owen Roe inflicted a crushing defeat on the Scots partly because their pikes were longer *'by a foot or two'*.

The ash stave was tapered in order to make it more balanced. Examination of pike staves in the Royal Armouries suggests that the butt is usually an inch in diameter. The thickest part, about an inch and a half in diameter is between a third and halfway towards the head after which point it narrows again to quite a small diameter, half an inch or less, where it enters the socket of the steel head. This tapering had one drawback which was described by Orrery, *'the slenderer part of the pike . . . is the more liable to be cut off'*. He, along with many other writers recommended that the end of the pike should be protected against this danger by long thin steel plates, known today as cheeks or langets. These plates also had the effect of strengthening the pike. Without them the pikes *are very apt to be broken off near the heads, if the push be vigorous and the resistance considerable'*. Orrery recommended that these plates should be

Figure 95
An illustration from Hexham's Principles of the Art Military.

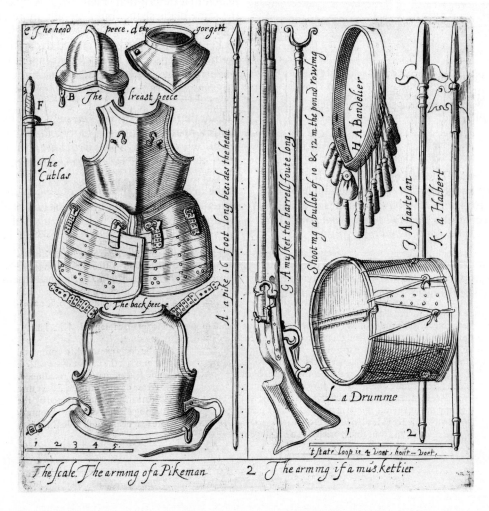

Figure 96
An illustration from de Gheyn's Wappenhandlung showing a Dutch pikehead.

enter, and when entered, broad to wound with'. It is uncertain whether Orrery means a lozenge-shaped cross-section or profile, although his comment that they are 'broad to wound with' suggests the latter. Hexham who had served in Holland illustrates a lozenge-shaped pike-head in his military manual (Figure 95). The pike heads illustrated by De Gheyn are of the same shape (Figure 96). A pike-head of this general form was found at Basing House, Hampshire (Figure 97), the scene of two sieges during the English Civil Wars, and another is in the Amsterdam Historisch Museum (Figure 98). An inventory of the stores in the Tower of London in 1634 refers to Dutch pikes with *'flatt heads'* suggesting that this lozenge-shape could be of Dutch origin.

The same document also described *'Long English pikes with square heads'* which in this case presumably refers to a diamond-shaped cross-section of the heads as opposed to the flat cross-section of the Dutch pike-heads. Also from Basing House comes another pike-head which could match that description (Figure 97). A pike-head of the same blade shape, but generally more ornate with baluster mouldings between the blade and socket and with blued and etched decoration on the blade, appears in a Dutch painting of the English soldier Sir John Burroughs in the Rijksmuseum in Amsterdam.

Yet another shape seems to be suggested by Monk in his *Observations upon Military and Political Affairs,* who refers to a *'small steel head'* and many other shapes survive in actual examples or illustrations. However, it does seem that the shape of the head was important although contemporary writers differ about which was best. At Benburb in Ireland in 1646 not only was the length of pikes a factor but the shape of the heads as well. The Irish pikes *'were far better to pierce being four square and small'* whilst the Scots pikes were *'broadheaded, which are the worst in the world'*, a statement which seems to contradict Orrery.

four feet long, although the usual length seems to have been about two feet. A contract made on 12 January 1654 with Anthony Webster, for 5,000 pikes specifies the *'bars to be strong and serviceable, in length two feete or two and twenty inches . . .'*

These bars were made as extensions of the socket of the head. Of the head itself Orrery recommends a lozenge-shaped head *'because they are sharp to*

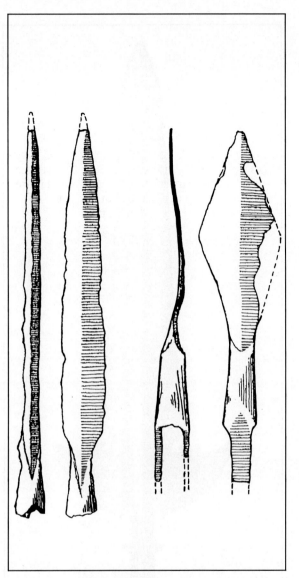

Figure 97
Two pikeheads excavated at Basing
House which was destroyed in 1645.
S. Moorhouse

Figure 98
A Dutch pikehead.
Amsterdams Historisches Museum.

Halberds and Partisans

The two most common staff-weapons in use during the English Civil Wars, apart from the pike, were the partisan and the halberd. Writing in 1622 Francis Markham described these as the weapons of officers and sergeants respectively. Even at this date however the use of the partisan by Captains was falling into disuse, many prefering to use what Markham calls a feather-staff, better known as a leading staff. By the time of the civil wars only lieutenants appear to have been using the partisan whilst the sergeants still retained the halberd. Monck wrote *'the Lieutenants and Sergeants ought to have Partizans and Halberts of eleven foot in length'*, and Elton wrote that the sergeant *'perceiving any Souldier out of order, he may cast in his Halbert between their Ranks, to cause him to march even abrest . . .'* This division of use is reflected in the supply of these weapons to the New Model Army whose regiments consisted of ten companies and would therefore have, generally, ten lieutenants and twenty sergeants. Thus in April 1645 we find Pickering's regiment, later Hewson's, being supplied with ten partisans and twenty halberds.

The partisan has a long broad blade surmounting two upturned flukes (Figure 99) whilst the halberd has a broad axe-like blade, with a down-turned fluke at its base surmounted by a long spike or a blade (Figure 100). The appearance of British partisans and halberds of this period is difficult to ascertain as there is a lack of any dated examples and pictorial evidence is similarly lacking. However, it does seem likely, if only because it is so common on staff-weapons found in this country, that heart-shaped piercings are an indication of British origins. This is borne out by halberds extant in the United States which were carried to America by British emigrants and have just such piercings. Another type of halberd which may well be British is represented by a group from the armoury at Farleigh Hungerford Castle (Figure 101).

Figure 99
A Partisan.
Royal Armouries VII 218.

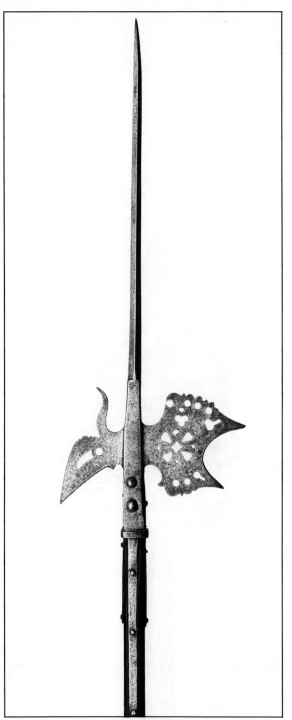

Figure 100
An English halberd with typical
heart-shaped piercings.
Royal Armouries VII 1521.

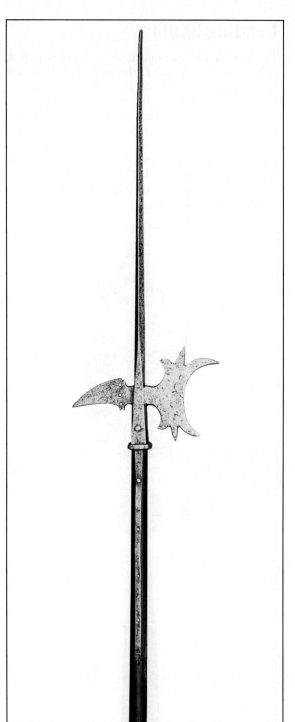

Figure 101
A halberd from the armoury of
Farleigh Hungerford Castle.
Royal Armouries VII 1809.

Leading Staffs

The leading staff mentioned above is not strictly a weapon at all, although at the Battle of Cheriton in 1644 a parliamentarian cavalry officer, Captain Fleming, was wounded by one. Interestingly the account of Cheriton which records this incident refers specifically to *'a captain's leading staff'* and indeed by this time it had become a recognised badge of rank for captains. Few leading staffs have survived to the present day but two fine and very different examples are preserved in the Royal Armouries (Figure 102).

Figure 102
Two captain's leading staffs.
Royal Armouries VII 229 and 230.

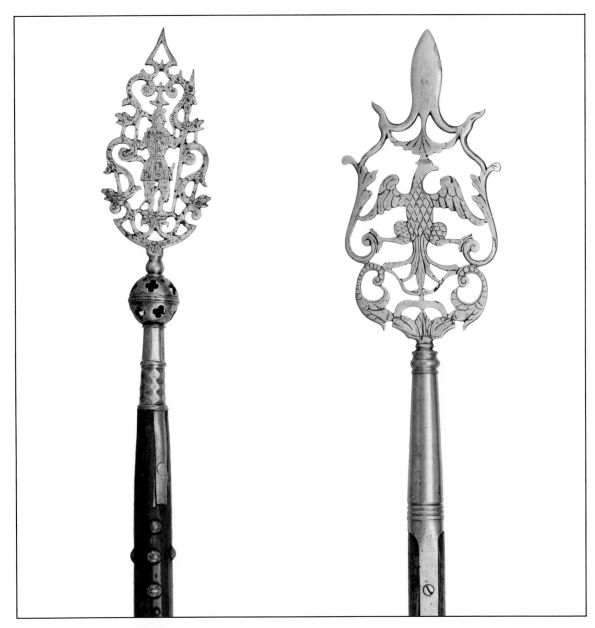

Bills

A staff-weapon used most frequently by the royalist forces was the bill (Figure 103). Originally an agricultural implement it bears a resemblance to the halberd with its long cutting edge and rear and top spikes. It appears to have been more frequently issued to troops in garrisons where a sixteen foot long pike would be of limited value. In December 1642 Charles I ordered that all available bills should be sent to the garrison of Reading. Bills were also used on several occasions by the defenders of Basing House in sallies against the besiegers. It is also possible however that bills were used by the royalists to compensate for a lack of more conventional staff weapons.

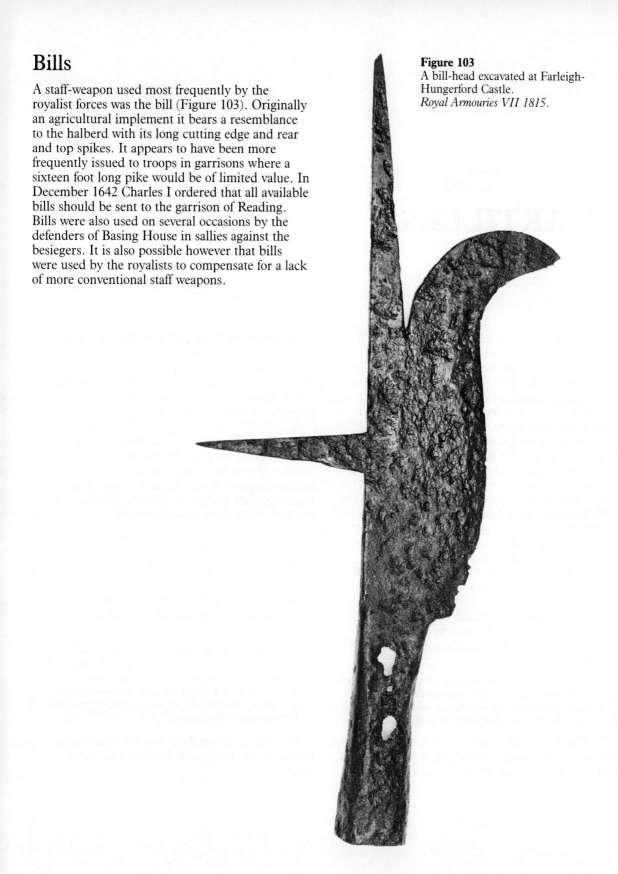

Figure 103
A bill-head excavated at Farleigh-Hungerford Castle.
Royal Armouries VII 1815.

The
ARTILLERY

The artillery in use during the English Civil Wars can be broadly divided into two types; siege artillery and field artillery. Both together made up an army's train of artillery. Great importance was attached to having an effective train although it was something of a bottomless pit for eating up resources. Clarendon, bemoaning the King's inadequate train before Edgehill, wrote that it *'is a spunge that can never be filled or satisfied'*. Yet generals would not do without the most effective train they could have. Essex, in 1643, when marching to the relief of Gloucester, was urged by Parliament to leave behind his heavier guns for the sake of speed. He refused. The importance Essex attached to having an effective train can further be seen by the fact that when he surrendered at Lostwithiel he lost his entire train including *'49 pieces of fair brass ordnance'*.

The reasons for this concern with artillery can most clearly be seen in accounts of sieges. At Sherborne Fairfax battered the castle with his siege artillery to great effect,

> *'The great Guns began to play about eleven of the clock, and before six had made a breach in the middle of the wall, that ten a breast might enter, and had beaten down one of the Towers which much disheartened the enemy.'*

At Winchester the siege artillery made in one day a breach wide enough for thirty men abreast to enter. The following day the royalist garrison surrendered. At Tiverton the artillery was also able to effect a breach in the royalists defences albeit in an unusual manner. A ball from the guns firing at the towns defences snapped the chain of the drawbridge which then fell, allowing the parliamentarians to enter the town.

On the battlefield, however, artillery met with mixed success. At Edgehill and Marston Moor the artillery of both sides made opening bombardments but once battle was joined the guns were effectively useless. At Naseby Fairfax's artillery hardly came into play at all.

> *'Being come within canon-shot the Ordnance began to play, but that being found at Marston Moor and other places but a losse of time, we resolved not to want any daylight, as is usual, but to charge with the first'*.

Soon afterwards, however, at the Battle of Langport the artillery played a crucial role. Sprigge describes how

> *'our Ordnance began to play (a good while before the foot engaged) doing great execution upon the body of the enemies Army, both horse and foot, who stood in good order upon the hill (about musquet shot from the passe) and forcing them to draw off their Ordnance, and their horse to remove their ground'*.

It was without doubt this action that enabled the parliamentary horse to make their successful attack.

CANNON

During the seventeeth century, cannon were not known by the weight of the shot they fired nor by the diameter of their bore. Rather each size of cannon had a name, the largest being the 63pdr cannon royal followed by the 47pdr whole cannon, and the 27pdr demi-cannon, the 15pdr culverin and 9pdr demi culverin, the 5¼pdr saker, the 4pdr minion, the 2¼pdr falcon and the 1¼pdr falconet, the ¾pdr robinet and, the smallest, the ½pdr base. However, many authors of works on artillery add other sub-divisions of these basic types. Thus Nathaniel Nye in his book *The Art of Gunnery* lists the great culverin, ordinary culverin and small culverin. The picture is further confused by the use of drakes. These were shorter, lighter versions of the standard sizes of cannon and used a smaller charge of powder. Robert Norton in his *Gunners Dialogue* gives the length of a saker as 10½ feet as against the 5¼ feet of the saker-drake, the powder charges being 5¼lb and 2lb respectively. A further feature of the drake was that the bore tapered at the breech end. In addition to the drake versions of the standard cannon there was also a group of drakes which were identified by the weight of shot fired. These are described by Hexham as being 3, 6, 12 and 24pdrs.

The largest sizes of artillery, the cannons and culverins, were generally reserved for siege work. Charles I's train of artillery, which was captured at Naseby, included two demi-cannon and a culverin which had earlier been used at the siege of Leicester; they were used there again by the New Model Army when it was recaptured from the royalists. When Cromwell attacked Basing House in 1645 he employed two demi-cannon and a whole cannon whilst the provisions for the proposed siege of Oxford, also in 1645, included two demi-cannons and three whole culverins. At Sherborne, Fairfax used whole cannon and demi-cannon.

Demi-culverins and the smaller guns were the field pieces of the day and of these the most commonly used was the saker. In addition to his siege artillery

Figure 104
Bronze 4 pdr cannon cast in 1638 by John Browne.
Royal Armouries XIX 170.

Figure 105
A gun cast for Charles I when a
prince by John Browne.
Royal Armouries XIX 24.

Figure 106
A gun cast for Charles I when a
prince by Thomas Pitt.
Royal Armouries XIX 29.

the king lost eight sakers at Naseby. Fairfax's train at the same battle included only two demi-culverins but also eight sakers, one long saker and three saker-drakes. At the second battle of Newbury in 1644 six out of nine brass guns captured by Essex's infantry were sakers. Also in common use were the three pound and six pound drakes. Prior to the establishment of the New Model Army, during the winter of 1644-5, a new army was proposed for the Earl of Essex. The warrant for the new train of artillery lists no fewer than fourteen drakes, of which at least two were six pounders, and in the north of England Lord Fairfax was using 3pdr drakes. A list for a royalist train of artillery of 1644 also contains reference to 3pdr and 6pdr cannon.

When studying English artillery pieces of this period two names stand out above all others, John Browne and Thomas Pitt. John Browne was a member of a family of Wealden ironfounders based at Horsmonden in Kent, although he had another foundry at Brenchley, also in Kent. In the mid 1620's the biggest market for cannon was the navy which preferred cannon cast in brass because they were lighter than their cast-iron equivalents. In fact the metal used was actually bronze but it was always referred to as brass. In order to try to obtain some of that market Browne experimented with the production of lightweight cast-iron guns, including the manufacture of drakes. So successful was he that in 1627 he received an order for four demi-cannon, sixteen culverins and one hundred and twenty demi-culverins, all to be cast-iron drakes.

His success was a challenge to Pitt who was a founder of brass cannon in Houndsditch, London, and who was spurred on to attempt to reduce the weight of his brass cannon below that of the new drakes. Then in a further challenge Browne started to cast brass cannon at Horsmonden and later at Brenchley. It was probably at one of these two foundries that Charles I witnessed the casting of a brass gun in 1638. This gun is now part of the collection of the Royal Armouries along with another almost identical gun, (Figure 104) whilst yet another of the same pattern is in the Guildhall Museum in Boston, Lincolnshire.

During the wars Browne supplied guns to the parliamentarian cause, although his loyalties appear to have been to Charles I; he was suspected of having supplied guns to the king during the early part of the wars. It was during the years 1638 and 1639 that Browne and Pitt supplied a number

Figure 107
Dutch brass gun.
Guildhall Museum, Boston, Lincolnshire.

Figure 108.
Queen Elizabeth's pocket pistol at
Dover Castle. The carriage is
19th century.
Royal Armouries XIX 246.

of small brass pieces for Prince Charles, later
Charles II (Figures 105 and 106). Although
miniatures these guns are in the same style as full
size guns. It is recorded that in 1651 there were a
total of fifteen of these guns although now only ten
survive, five each by Browne and Pitt. However,
Pitt died in 1645 and after that the supply of both
cannon and roundshot was almost monopolised by
Browne.

Also preserved in the Guilhall Museum in Boston
is a brass Dutch cannon cast by Kylianus
Wegewart in 1630 (Figure 107). Kylianus and his
brother Conraet manufactured guns at the Dutch
National Foundry at The Hague from 1618 to
1664. Although slightly larger, firing a 3¾pdr shot,
it is probably very much like two 3pdr Dutch guns
that were used by the royalists in 1644.

Another Dutch gun is on loan from the Royal
Armouries to Dover Castle (Figure 108). This is a
12pdr gun which was cast in Utrecht in 1544, and
given to Henry VIII in 1545 by Maximillian van
Egmont, Count of Buren and Stadtholder of
Friesland. It was recorded as being at Dover Castle
as early as 1547, and William Eldred, the Master
Gunner of Dover Castle, carried out a practice
shoot with it in 1613. The gun was loaded with
eighteen pounds of powder, a ten pound ball and
given two degrees of elevation; the ball struck a
target twelve hundred yards away. Eldred
described this gun as a *'Basilisco'* because of its
great length, 24 feet, which makes it a very
impressive piece. During the civil wars the gun
was pressed into service as part of the Earl of
Essex's train of artillery and was captured by the
royalists at Lostwithiel in 1644. At the end of the
wars the gun was returned to Dover Castle where
it has become known as Queen Elizabeth's Pocket
Pistol.

Gun Carriages

Prominent amongst the ordnance records of this period are frequent orders for gun carriages. For example, in April 1645 Thomas Bateman, John Pitt and Thomas Hodgskin supplied gun carriages for two demi-culverins and eight sakers to equip Fairfax's artillery. The construction of a gun carriage was a complicated affair. Different sorts of wood were used for different parts; Hexham states that the cheeks or side-pieces of a carriage and the wheels were to be made of elm, while the axle trees and spokes were to be oak. The size of gun carriages was also carefully regulated, all the various parts being made in proportion to the dimensions of the barrel. An edition of Richard Elton's *Compleat Body of the Art Military,* published in 1668 contains a supplement written by Captain Thomas Rudd, who is described as chief engineer to Charles I. In this supplement Rudd states that a carriage should be one and a half times as long as the length of the bore of a gun, and that the planks at the fore-end of a carriage should be four times the diameter of the bore in deep and the same as the diameter of the bore in thickness. The wheels, generally, should be half the length of the barrel in diameter, although this rule is amended for the smaller sizes of guns. The dimensions of every piece of a carriage is given in this manner.

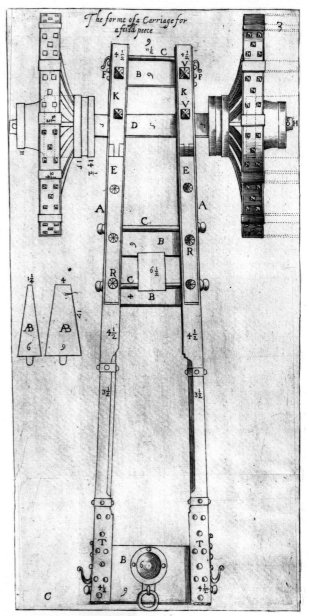

Figure 109
Drawing of a gun carriage from Hexham's Principles of the Art Military.

MORTARS

In addition to the various cannon used in the English civil wars mortars were also employed. These are pieces with very short barrels and, in proportion, very wide bores designed to fire with a very high trajectory. These formed part of the siege artillery and were known by the size of their calibre in inches. In April 1645 John Phipps, Commissary to the New Model Army's train of artillery, received a 13in brass mortar from Manchester's disbanded train of artillery. At about the same time John Browne was contracted for a brass mortar of 8¼in. weighing 4cwt 0qtr 14lb whilst in August of the same year he supplied a brass 13in mortar weighing 10cwt 0qtr 2lb. Browne also supplied large quantities of 12½in mortar shells, many of which were delivered for use against Basing House. As far as is known only one mortar has survived from this period and that one is probably the most unusual of all mortars employed during the civil wars. Preserved in Hereford and known as Roaring Meg it is a rough cast-iron mortar cast locally by Colonel Birch for use at the seige of Goodrich Castle in 1646 (Figure 110). This mortar has a bore of 15in while one of its shells has a diameter of 13½in.

In using a mortar the object was to drop a shell onto the target using the high trajectory of this type of artillery. The mortar shell itself was a hollow iron sphere filled with powder with a slow burning fuse intended to ignite the powder as the shell landed. As the fuse in the shell had to be lit before the mortar could be fired it was a rather risky business requiring great skill and timing. In the hands of a skilled gunner, however, the mortar was a devastating weapon. Such a man was Thomas Wrightwho served at the seige of Elizabeth Castle on Jersey in 1651, and he describes vividly the effect of one shot he made,

> '. . . this shot strike quite through the Roof of the Church, and fell into a Warehouse underneath the Church, where the Enemy had their Magazine of powder and other things, which by the Granados breaking there, it was all set on fire, their Church thrown down, and many dwelling houses, totally ruinated by this blowe . . .'.

He goes on to detail the extent of death and destruction caused including *'sixteen or eighteen dead'*, and a great amount of provisions and stores destroyed.

Figure 110
The mortar 'Roaring Meg' on a modern bed at Hereford.
Hereford Museums and Art Gallery.

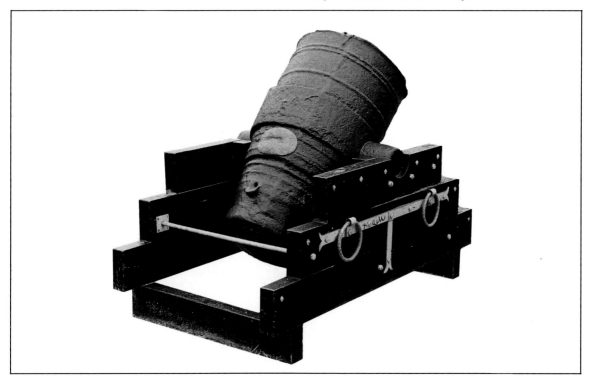

LEATHER GUNS

Perhaps the oddest type of ordnance used in the civil wars was the leather cannon (Figures 111 and 112). These guns had originated in Switzerland in 1622 and were subsequently introduced into Sweden in 1627 by an Austrian called Melchio Wurmbrandt who constructed leather guns for Gustavus Adolphus. Although eventually replaced in Gustavus's army by lightweight all-metal guns the idea was brought to England in 1629 by Colonel Robert Scott. Scott died in 1631, but his nephew, Colonel James Wemyss, carried on working on the development of these guns and was appointed master gunner of England in 1638.

Wemyss subsequently became Sir William Waller's Lieutenant-General of Ordnance and joined Waller's army in December 1643, taking a number

of his leather cannon with him. A contemporary observer noted:

> 'These leather pieces are of very great use, and very easie and light of carriage. One horse may draw a peece, which will carry a bullet of a pound and halfe weight, and doe execution very farre'.

At Cropredy Bridge, however, the following year Wemyss and much of Waller's artillery were captured including '2 Barricadoes of wood drawn with wheeles in each 7 small brasse & leather Gunns charged with case shott'. Wemyss continued to make leather cannon in Scotland; some of which were probably captured with Wemyss at the Battle of Worcester in 1651 in the service of Charles II. Wemyss finally died in 1667 after once again being appointed master gunner of England in 1661, following the restoration of the monarchy.

Twenty-three leather guns, probably all made by Wemyss, survive in collections in Scotland, being mounted singly, in pairs and in fours. In England, a single example at the Museum of Artillery, the Rotunda, Woolwich, two more guns in the Museum of Artillery, Paris and one more in the Zeughaus, Berlin all have dolphins in the shape of a letter G and are thought to have belonged to the army of Gustavus Adolphus.

Figure 111
Scottish leather cannon.
National Museums of Scotland.

Wemyss leather guns do, however, differ from the guns of Gustavus Adolphus. Wemyss guns are much shorter in proportion and consequently much lighter. There are also constructional differences. Wemyss's guns have at their core an iron tube strengthened by irons rings and closed at the breech-end by and iron plug. The barrels were then bound in hemp before being covered with a leather coat sewn up along the underside of the barrels. The touch-holes pass down into the barrels from the top of the gun as with a conventional cannon barrel.

Examination of the leather gun at the Rotunda has revealed several differences in construction. It has a copper tube which has been reinforced by having white or tinned iron wire wrapped around it. Four wooden lathes running the length of the gun were then bound to it by hemp binding and metal collars. The binding was set in plaster of paris, and the whole thing covered in leather. The breech arrangement is also more complex than that of the Scottish guns, with a conical breech casting that fits into the tapered end of the copper tube and also contains a touch-hole in the axis of the barrel and a flash pan on the rear face of the breech.

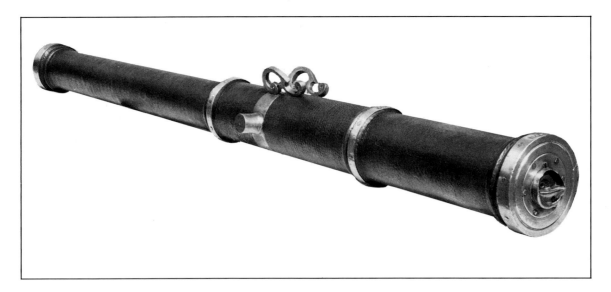

Figure 112
A Swedish leather cannon.
Royal Artillery Institute.

ACCESSORIES

All cannon, whether iron, brass or leather, required the same tools to load and fire them. These were the ladle, rammer, sponge, wadhook and linstock (Figures 113 and 114). The ladle was a long trowel like shovel which was used for loading loose powder into a gun. Made of copper or brass to avoid any possibility of sparks its size was carefully regulated so that it acted as a measure to ensure the correct amount of powder was loaded. The use of loose powder, however, was recognised as a dangerous practice and during the middle part of the seventeenth century there was an increased use of cartridges. These were cylindrical bags of cloth or paper that held the correct charge for a particular size of cannon. The rammer was used to ram home the powder and shot before firing, and the sponge, made from a cylinder of wood covered in sheepskin, was soaked in water and thrust down the barrel after firing to extinguish any burning fragments left in the gun before it was reloaded. The wadhook was used to extract any debris from the barrel or to pull out charges to unload the gun. The linstock was a long pole with a clamp at the end which held the slow-match that a gunner used to ignite the powder in the touch-hole of the gun and so fire it. These often have two clamps and can be quite ornate.

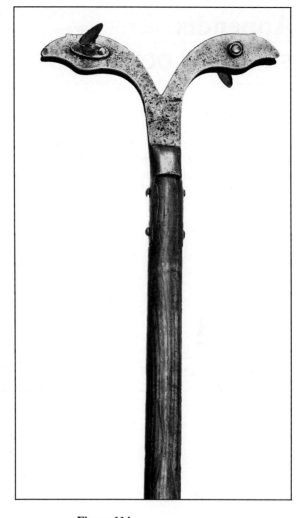

Figure 113
An illustration of artillery tools from an Italian artillery manual by Thomaso Moretti.

Figure 114
An artillery linstock.
Royal Armouries VII 1152.

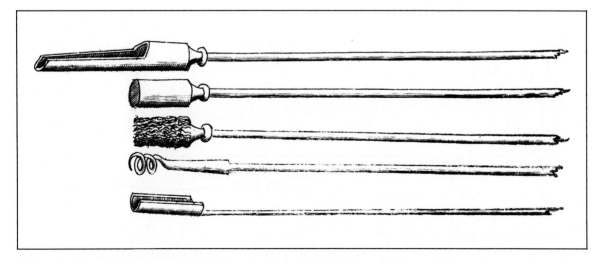

Appendix
FIREARM LOCK TYPES

Matchlocks

There are two forms of matchlock, the older sear-lock (Figure 115) and the trigger-lock (Figure 116) which by the time of the English Civil Wars had superseded the sear-lock although no doubt some of those were still in use. In the case of the sear-lock upward pressure on the lever (1) under the butt pivoted a lever (2) against the action of a spring (3) which pulled down a tumbler (4) causing the cock (5) to move towards the pan. The end of the cock was formed as a clamp and held a length of slow burning cord or match. This ignited a small priming charge of gun-powder in the pan which in turn ignited the main charge in the barrel through the touch-hole. With the trigger-lock pulling the trigger exerted a similar pressure on a pivoted lever (1), again against the action of a spring (2) and with the same result.

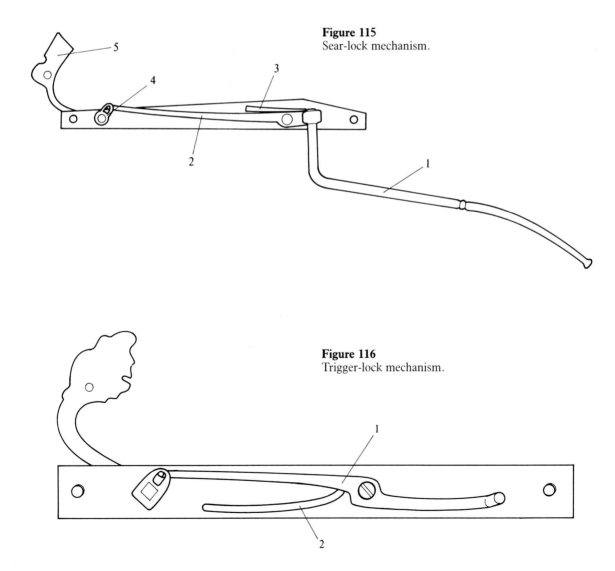

Figure 115
Sear-lock mechanism.

Figure 116
Trigger-lock mechanism.

Wheellocks

The wheellock (Figure 117) produces the spark necessary to ignite the primary charge in the pan by means of a serrated wheel spinning against a piece of pyrites held in the jaws of a cock. The wheel is powered by a strong V-shaped spring (1) connected to the wheel by a chain (2). When the wheel is wound up, or spanned, the spring is compressed and a laterally acting sear (3), passing through the lock-plate, engages in a hole on the inside of the wheel, thus holding the mechanism in the spanned position. The edge of the serrated wheel protrudes into the bottom of the priming pan (4) which has a sliding cover. To fire the gun the cock (5) is lowered until the pyrites is resting on the pan cover (6), held down by the force of another spring. On pulling the trigger the sear disengages from the wheel allowing it to revolve, at the same time the pan cover is automatically slid out of the way causing the pyrites to come into contact with the revolving wheel sending a shower of sparks into the pan.

Figure 117
Wheellock mechanism.

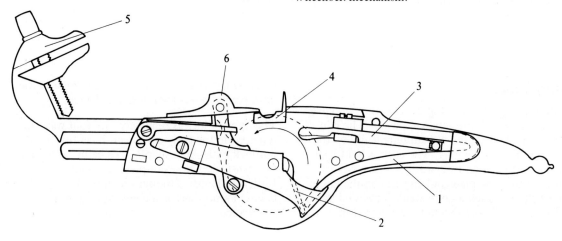

Flintlocks

In the case of the flintlock the spark to ignite the priming-charge is produced by the action of a piece of flint, held in the jaws of the cock, striking against a piece of steel known as the frizzle. The frizzle is placed above the pan and as the flint strikes it, knocking it away, a shower of sparks is produced.

During the period of the English Civil Wars there were a number of different locks in use which might be called flintlocks. These were referred to without distinction as snaphances, a term today applied to one particular form of flintlock with a separate frizzle and pan-cover. The term snaphance, when used in contemporary documents, however, generally refers to the later developments of the flintlock which have the frizzle and pan-cover in one piece. Today these are generally referred to as English-locks.

In 1984 the author and his colleague, Mr Graeme Rimer, visited Littlecote House in order to catalogue the firearms in that collection. In the course of their work they were able to remove the locks from nearly every flintlock arm in order to study the mechanism. This resulted in the discovery of five distinct lock types which are described below. Only types 1 to 4 were found on muskets, and, whilst both types 1 and 2 were found on pistols, the commonest pistol-lock was type 5. The well-known Littlecote 'carbines' all have type 5 locks. It must be stressed that no chronological progression is implied by this typology.

Snaphance

With this type of lock (Figure 118) the pan cover (1) and frizzle (2) are separate pieces. The pan cover is slid out of the way automatically by the action of the cock falling. The cock is held back in the cocked position by a sear (3) which passes through the lock-plate and engages on the tail of the cock (4) , often a dog-catch is provided as a safety-catch. Before the gun can be fired the separate frizzle (2) has to be pulled down to the flash pan which is itself a safety device.

This type of lock is relatively rare as it was quickly replaced in the early seventeenth century by the flintlock with some snaphances being converted to English-locks. No examples were found at Littlecote House although the flintlock type 3 (see below) found there is a conversion from the snaphance.

Figure 118
Snaphance mechanism.

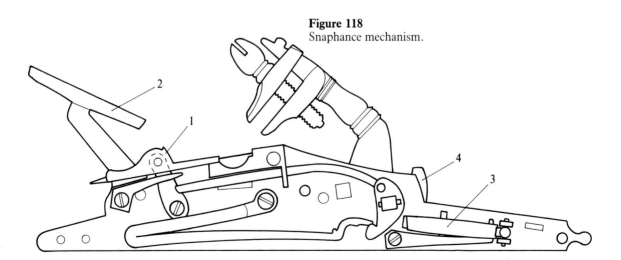

Type 1

This type of English-lock (Figure 119) has two positions for the cock, half-cock and full-cock. It is held at full cock by a lug (1) on the laterally operating sear (2) which projects through the lockplate and engages on the tail of the cock (3), and at half-cock by the angled nose of the sear (4), which lodges on the rear of a wedge-shaped lug (5) on the underside of the tumbler.

The purpose of the half-cock position, in which it cannot be fired, is to allow the combined frizzle and pan cover (6) to be shut without having to fully cock the gun ready for firing. This type of lock was found with and without an additional dog-catch.

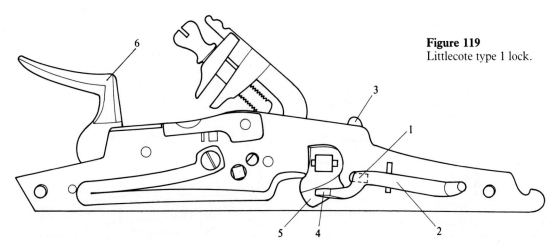

Figure 119
Littlecote type 1 lock.

Type 2

This lock, (Figure 120) is similar to Type 1, but has a sear (1) with the nose cut with a vertical V-shaped notch in order that it should lodge over the angled rear edge of the lug (2) beneath the tumbler. This type of lock was also found with and without a dog-catch.

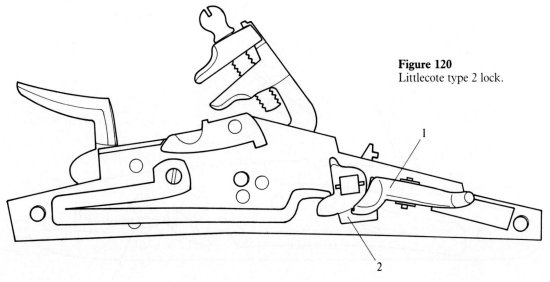

Figure 120
Littlecote type 2 lock.

Type 3

This lock, (Figure 121) has a two-piece laterally operating sear (1) which resembles that of a wheellock, and which is fitted with a dog catch (2) for the half-cock position. Interestingly two examples of this type were found which were clearly converted snaphance locks.

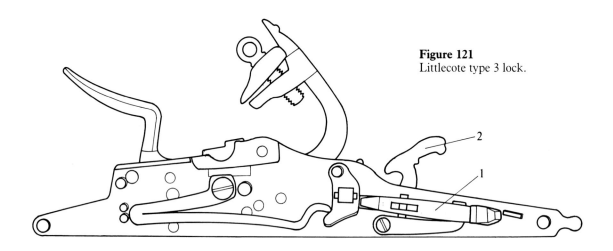

Figure 121
Littlecote type 3 lock.

Type 4

This type of lock, (Figure 122) has a laterally operating one-piece sear (1). The lock is held at half-cock by means of a dog catch (2), and at full-cock by the nose of the sear engaging over the rear surface of a wedge-shaped lug (3) on the rear of the tumbler.

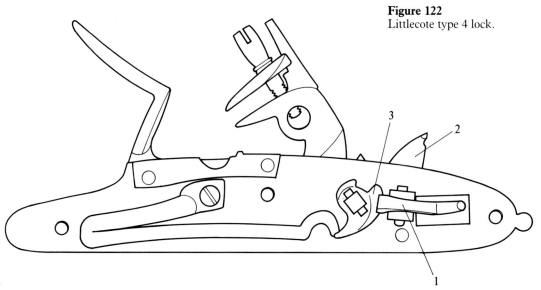

Figure 122
Littlecote type 4 lock.

Type 5

This lock, (Figure 123) has a laterally operating two-function sear (1). The lock is held at half-cock by a long limb on the sear (2) which curves around the upper part of the tumbler and hooks over a wedge-shaped lug (3), and at full-cock by a small angled face at the root of the half-cock limb (5) which engages over a second smaller wedge-shaped projection (4) on the rear of the tumbler. Interestingly in some of the Littlecote examples additional safety is achieved not by a dog catch but by a small pivoting lever lying beneath the cock which can engage a notch on its lower edge. This rather feeble device was automatically cammed out of engagement by a carefully arranged curve to the rear of this notch, which allowed the cock to fall unhindered after being raised to the fully-cocked position.

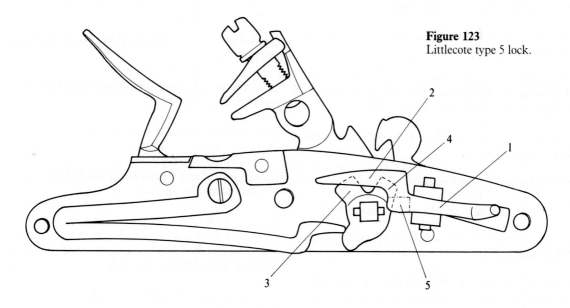

Figure 123
Littlecote type 5 lock.

Figure 115-123
All illustrations by Hugh Tisdale

Bibliography

Adair, John (ed) **They Saw it Happen** *Hampshire* 1981

Adair, John **By the Sword Divided** *London* 1983

Barrife, William **Militaire Discipline** *London* 1661

Blackmore, Howard L **British Military Firearms** *London* 1961

Blackmore, Howard L **The Armouries of the Tower of London** *Vol I* **Ordnance** 1976

Blackmore, Howard L **A Dictionary of London Gunmakers** *London* 1986

Blair, Claude (ed David H Caldwell) **The Early Basket-Hilt in** Britain **Scottish Weapons and Fortification 1100-1800** *Edinburgh* 1981

Brown, Rodney Hilton **American Polearms 1526-1865** *Connecticut* 1967

Bull, Stephen **Granadoe** 1986

Bullstrode, Sir Richard **Memoirs** *London* 1721

Carlyle, Thomas **Letters and Speeches of Oliver Cromwell** 1845

Clarendon, Earl of (ed W D Macray) **History of the Rebellion and Civil Wars in England** *6 vols* 1888

Cleere H and Crossley D **The Iron Industry of the Weald** 1985

Cruso, J C **Militaire Instructions for the Cavallrie** *Cambridge* 1632

De Gheyn, Jacob **Exercise of Arms** 1607

Eldred, William **The Gunners Glasse** *London* 1646

Firth, C H **Cromwell's Army** *London* 1962

Garner, A A **Boston and the Great Civil War** 1972

Goodwin, Rev G N **The Civil War in Hampshire** 1904

Hexham, Henry **Principles of the Art Military** *Holland* 1642

Hodgson, John **Life of Captain Hodgson** *London* 1882

Hutchinson, Lucy **Memoirs of the Life of Colonel Hutchinson** 1968

Lewendon, Brig R J **The Leather Gun of Gustavus Adolphus of Sweden in the Rotunda Collection at Woolwich** The Journal of the Royal Artillery Vol CXII March 1985

Lytton Sells, A (ed) **The Memoirs of James II** *Indiana* 1962

Markham, Francis **Five Decades of Epistles of Warre** *London* 1622

Markham, Gervase **Souldiers Accidence** *London* 1625

Monck, George, Duke of Albemarle **Observations upon Military and Political Affairs** *London* 1671

Moorhouse, Stephen, **Finds from Basing House, Hampshire, (c1540-1645): Part Two,** Post Medieval Archaeology, Vol 5. 1971

Moretti; Thomaso **Trattato dell'Artigliera** *Venice* 1665

Mungeam, Gerald **Contracts for the Supply of Equipment to the New Model Army in 1645** Journal of the Arms and Armour Society Vol VI No 3

Newman, Dr Peter **The Battle of Marston Moor** *Chichester* 1981

Norman, A V B **The Rapier and Small Sword 1460-1820** *London* 1980

Orrery, Roger, Earl of **A Treatise of the Art of War** *London* 1677

Parthenope, Frances, Lady Verney **Memoirs of the Verney Family** *London* 1925

Peachey, S and Turton, A **Old Robins Foot** 1987

Peterson, Harold L **Encyclopaedia of Firearms** *London* 1964

Rushworth, John **Historical Collections** *7 vols* 1654-1701

Scott, Sir Sibbald David, Bt, **The British Army, Its Origin, Progress and Equipment,** *London* 1868

Sprigge, Josiah **Anglia Rediviva** *London* 1647

Stevenson, D and Caldwell, D H **Leather Guns and Other Light Artillery in Mid-Seventeenth Century Scotland** 1977

Thomason Tracts British Library

Toynbee, M and Young, P **Cropredy Bridge 1644** *Kineton* 1970

Turner, Sir James **Pallas Armata** *London* 1683

Vernon, John **The Young Horseman** *London* 1644

Walker, Sir Edward **Historical Discourses** 1705

Young, Peter **Naseby** 1985

Young, Peter and Tucker, N **Richard Atkins and John Gwyn** 1967

Published State Papers:
Calendar of State Papers, Domestic, Charles I

Unpublished State Papers:
SP 16/179
SP 23/131, 29, 30
WO 47/61, 64
WO 55/1646,1690, 483, 1662
PRO 30/37